MW01142392

WORLD FOODS
— WITH —
STRANGE NAMES

DR. IAN GRIERSON

authorHOUSE®

AuthorHouse™ UK
1663 Liberty Drive
Bloomington, IN 47403 USA
www.authorhouse.co.uk
Phone: UK TFN: 0800 0148641 (Toll Free inside the UK)
*   UK Local: (02) 0369 56322 (+44 20 3695 6322 from outside the UK)*

Published by AuthorHouse 07/20/2022

ISBN: 978-1-7283-7429-1 (sc)
ISBN: 978-1-7283-7428-4 (e)

CONTENTS

INTRODUCTION

I got the idea for this collection of oddly named dishes while I was writing books on where our favourite foods actually originated. During my life I have travelled a lot on most Continents both for work and pleasure. I always have had an interest in the local foods and classic dishes of different countries; as a result my life style suited my passion. You might say each feeding off the other (sorry about that I have a poor sense of humour).

The names of dishes are most often purely descriptive and say exactly what you will get. Take for example our British "fish and chips", Indian "sag aloo" (spinach and potato curry), Chinese "lin-moun chi" (lemon chicken), German "bratwurst mit sauerkraut" (sausage with sauerkraut) and so on. Dishes sometimes are called after the country where they originate for example "Irish Stew", "Russian salad" and "Swedish meatballs". Quite often they keep their regional names such as "gasconade de gigot d'agneau" ("Gascon leg of lamb"), "murg Kashmiri" ("Kashmir chicken"), "Florida grapefruit salad" and "Yorkshire puddings". Some foods even generate a high level of local pride so that they keep their hometown associations. Such is the case with "bistecca alla Florentina" ("Florence steak"), "Paella de Valencia"

(Valencian rice dish), "Finnan haddock" from northern Scotland and "Bath Buns" from the south west of England.

Given all that already said about names of dishes, World wide there are a number of foods that are distinguished by having odd names, often nothing at all to do with the constituents of the recipe. The name of the item might be a foodie joke as is the case I suppose with "spotted dick" the British currant steamed pudding that older relatives once thrived on. How about "croque monsieur" the classic French ham and cheese toastie that roughly converts into English as "Mister crunch"? On the other hand a Chinese dinner called "fuqi feipian" translates literally to "husband and wife lung slices" - nasty! Before any cannibals get too excited this spicy Sichuan street food was invented by a husband and wife duo from the 1930s who originally did use ox lung but these days it is mixed meat and other offal.

It is these dishes that particularly interest me and bring a smile to my face. If you want to find weird names for dishes then you needn't look much further than Britain and our traditional cuisine. China gives us a run for our money in terms of bizarre names dotted around its various cuisines while in addition USA contributes its fare share. The Americans also like to add foodie geographic confusion to the mix in their own inimitable way. What I mean is their "French fries" are actually Belgian, you can't get "Canadian bacon" in Canada because it is a term specific to the US, "Chinese fortune cookies" were created in California by Japanese immigrants so not at all Chinese - and so it goes on.

Crazy named dishes are not restricted to the three countries I've mentioned up to now - they merely excel at the silly name business while many others also compete quite effectively but to a slightly lesser degree of madness. When you dig deep into cuisines from around the World they all have a few dishes whose names are worth a giggle or two. I admit freely I have not trolled my way through the cuisines of the approximately 195 countries that make up the planet - I'm not that sad - nearly but not quite! I start with the UK and Ireland, go round Europe and countries in various Continents ending up in Canada following no good geographical progression what so ever. The countries I have chosen are places where I have been or I am comfortable with their cuisines so I selected a total of 28 countries while a further 18 selections are groups of related countries.

When it comes down to the 28 countries, I am familiar with the traditional dishes of all of those. Further I have grouped a bunch of countries together either because I think their dishes have a considerable overlap such as in the Caribbean Islands or as is the case for the bulk of Africa, I am not all that familiar with their traditional or even modern dishes. I have travelled extensively in North Africa but not so much elsewhere in that Continent. There are some 18 combinations of countries based on my convenience or ignorance so making a grand total of 46 sections each with 3 or 4 odd-named foods from the various countries' cuisines.

These are stories about foods and dishes, I haven't set out to write a recipe book though many of the dishes are yummy. I say yummy because I have either eaten the dish in a restaurant or made it at home. There are a few that I have only heard about and never had. Some are just revolting and if you read on you will know those ones immediately others are revolting just to me (for example Swiss "salted sugar" - see later). There are a few others where I can't get a hold of the ingredients. These are very few so the vast majority are reasonably well known to me and for the most part much enjoyed. However my object is to explain the food or dish and explore how they got such strange names. Yes it is by any foody terms a quirky approach but interesting to some of you I hope!

ENGLAND

1. **Periwinkles** - are intertidal sea snails that live on rocks grazing on algae. They are by no means restricted to British shores as they are around most of the European coastline. They even have made it to America where they are classed as an invasive species. Presumably they crossed the Atlantic from East to West in much the same way as we did but outside not inside the ship. Periwinkle snails are not ours but on these shores we were responsible for giving them such a bizarre name. To add complication to the story a periwinkle is in addition a European ground cover plant that also made the transatlantic trip to North America maybe not on the hull of a boat like its mollusc namesake. I know it as a big leafed plant with delicate blue flowers but there are seemingly all sort of different varieties throughout Europe so the flowers also can be white or purple it seems. Now you can't eat the plant, these periwinkles are quite poisonous but the molluscs on the other hand make good eating. Take your 'winkles and put them in a pot of boiling salted water for a little over five minutes. Now if you are of a certain age you will know of "winkle pickers" but as a pair of long, thin pointy shoes worn

by "Teddy Boys" in the 1950s. My winkle pickers are the necessary means by which you get your winkle out of its shell! Back in the day in my local pub on a Friday night the seafood man would arrive with polystyrene pots of this and that ranging from shrimps to rollmop herrings. My pals and I bought something because it was a tradition. I usually had prawns in their shells, someone else would have mussels but big Gordon always went for the boiled periwinkles. He would be offered a toothpick (winkle picker number one) but refused. He would take his winkle to the lips and with a terrible in take of breath the meat was vacuumed into his mouth (winkle picker number two). The pub clientele soon had enough of this horrible sucking sound so Gordon resorted to winkle picker number three, a rather dubious looking pin from the lapel of his jacket that had lived there for years or as far back as I could remember. A pin is a decent way to prize out the snail meat but best to use a fresh sterilized one. Sometime in the late 1990s our seafood man put his tray down for the last time and retired and so another tradition was lost. Never the most popular of seafood, periwinkles are rarely seen these days. However you still can get boiled winkles from fishmongers especially in seaside towns or they can be got on line. They are worth the effort with toothpick or pin and taste rather nice.

2. **Sweetbreads** - Sweetmeats sound like something cooked on the barbeque that comes off dripping in honey-rich marinade like pork ribs or some such. Of course no one uses the term sweetmeats these

days because sweetmeat is an outdated name for confectionary and sugary treats of various types. So the term has nothing at all to do with meat sweet or otherwise. Therefore I guess sweetbreads, in the same vein, are not sticky buns or bread loaves? Absolutely correct, sweetbreads come from the insides of various domestic beasts. So, lets get it right, sweetmeat is nothing to do with animal flesh of any type whereas sweetbread is "organ meat" as the Americans call it but we prefer the name "offal". At one time in our history, certainly up to the 19th Century and beyond, offal was prized and considered the prime pick of meats. Kidneys reigned supreme on the breakfast buffet menu of the well off, while liver in the form of pate or otherwise was a dinner starter classic. Perhaps other offal was less popular with the upper classes but still enjoyed by the general public such as brains, tripe and heart. Sweetbreads are not just one type of offal but a range of organs including pancreas (makes digestive enzymes and hormones like insulin) and thymus (helps fight infection) in particular. Sweetbreads I understand are so called because they were considered richer (or sweeter) than more conventional meat products. In addition *"British Food a History"* on line states "they are *bread* because the old English word for flesh is *bræd*." Most sweetbreads are from lamb or calf and are great fried up with bacon and served with a green vegetable. Additionally *"Jane Grigson"* in her masterful book *"Good Things"* pointed out that English sweetbreads and bacon are ideally paired with bread sauce.

3. **Fish Fingers** - fish have fins but do not have fingers except try telling that to the British public who eat their way through 1.5 million of them every day! Of course the fish finger came into being not at sea but in the *Birds Eye* factory in Great Yarmouth, Norfolk back in the mid 1950s. Indeed it was the workers themselves at their Great Yarmouth Factory who named the product fish fingers. That name has stuck and it is used in most countries from Germany to Australia. The exception being the USA who first came up with the idea back in the 1920s and 30s of taking slivers of white fish and coating the with breadcrumbs for frying. To this day they refer to these as fish sticks but in essence they are the same as fish fingers. The founder of the many *Birds Eye* factories around the World was *Clarence Birdseye* who created the frozen foods industry that blossomed first in America then elsewhere. As a result fish fingers come in boxes located in the freezer section of the supermarket. Taken together with frozen chips, garden peas and a big squirt of sauce you have one of the classic freezer meals of the 20th and 21st Centuries. Where ever fish fingers and sticks are eaten in the World the dish is made of white fish but may well differ in species depending on the country. The big International producer is not Great Yarmouth but a factory in the German Port of Bremerhaven, Germany. Fish fingers are popular in Germany and the factory supplies its home country's needs and exports to 20 others including Britain. This is factory production on a huge scale, nearly 3 billion fingers are manufactured per year at this one site. Fingers were produced originally

as a way of enticing children to eat fish. I don't think I ever tried them until my own children were clamoring for dinner in their early years. All I need do was to open the freezer and there they were, no heads, no tails and completely bland - perfect. No complaints about fishy smells nor sliminess; on with a dollop of ketchup and off we go dinner sorted (shame on me)! There is a price to pay fish fingers are a factory processed food like chicken nuggets (probably next days dinner) so they are not fillets but compressed white fish bits that I understand are mixed with chemicals and such like. They are more than a bit of a hazard to the factory workers also. I like the *"Paul O'Grady"* quote that goes "Noel Coward said work is more fun than fun, but then he didn't work in the Bird's Eye factory packing frozen fish fingers nine hours a day, did he?"

4. **Mucky Dripping** - We have a hole in our roof gutter that is strategically positioned above the front door. As a result when it rains, and for quite a while longer, we suffer from mucky drippings on the head going in or out. Yes I have promised to go up there and get it sorted but I am a wimp about heights. If you happen to be in the North of England, particularly Yorkshire, then your mucky drippings are indoors not outside! Not everywhere in doors but in the kitchen, specifically under a roast joint of beef. When you have formed a trivet with a few vegetables like sliced onion, carrot, parsnip and celery and placed your roast on top you are in business. As the meat cooks it glistens and drips fat and meaty juices into the underlying tray. This is

mucky dripping that with some fat scooped off, a little flour stirred in under heat, plus the addition of good stock then you have taken gravy to another level. Ok so mucky dripping is the stuff at the bottom of your roasting tray that adds flavour to gravies but what if you let it cool down and solidify? Then you have mucky fat that consists of white solid fat on the top that is made mucky by mixing it with the brown meaty jelly beneath. Stuff to get rid of but not to eat surely? Well hold on, here we have Northern pate to spread on bread or toast! Actually the fatty bit is very spreadable while the mucky bit is full of taste! Southern English might be rather aghast at spreading dripping fat on bread and eating it. However butter is also fat, and marginally less tasty, while margarine is a factory product that is far more ghastly than any natural fatty spread. Beef fats are used as spreads over bread throughout Europe. I can remember being beside Lake Balaton at a small vineyard in Hungary around 7am in the morning. Our generous hosts had us breakfasting with coffee, crisp breads smothered with herb flavoured dripping and on the side to finish off, dry sparkling white wine. A perfect view but had we been in Yorkshire the view would be equally brilliant, strong milky tca would be ideal, toast smeared thickly with mucky fat needs to be gobbled up when made available whether it be morning, noon or night but the boozing needs a modicum of control!

SCOTLAND

1. **Tipsy Laird** - this is Lowlands and Borders Scots speak but what is it all about? To be tipsy meant that you were more than a little drunk while lairds were mostly the local Estate owners that, in times past, required us ordinary people in Scotland to doff our caps to them whether we wanted to or not. Perhaps it was different further North in the Highlands but down South we were grateful for the almost perpetual absence of our "lairds" after all throughout history up to my time (that stretched to the mid 20th Century years) they kept the working classes away from their estates by using armed bailiffs and the constabulary. While our local farmers were mostly tenanted and denied ownership of the lands their forbearers had worked so diligently. There are not too many clues in this odd name so it would take a lot of guessing to get to the fact our tipsy laird is essentially the Scots version of trifle. Tipsy laird has a special place in the hierarchy of Scots desserts. It is the one you would have at a birthday party or an anniversary party. Many of the Burns supper celebrations on the 25th of January each year end up with a bowl of tipsy laird and our Scots trifle had pride of place on the buffet table

during Hogmanay (New Years Eve). It is a dish with an abundance of boozy sponge, plenty raspberry jam, lashings of custard, whipped cream and raspberries in abundance. There is no jelly, sprinkles and the like as with supermarket trifle while the more adult English versions contain sherry, Scots trifle has plenty whisky. Surprisingly, at least to me, whisky as an integral part of tipsy laird and is a relatively modern addition. Right up to the early 20th Century fortified wine or brandy did the job instead. Perhaps the dish is not so much different from its English cousin as we Scots like to claim?

2. **Crappit Heid** - what an awful name for anything never mind a dish that Scots people once ate. Often, but certainly not always, a yucky title disguises a delightful food. Sadly it is not the case in this instance. If I say Scots folks once did a lot of crapping, I am not talking about an outbreak of diarrhoea but stuffing meats and the like (the Scots meaning of the word) was often an important part of meal preparation. Crappit heid is Scots dialect for stuffed heads and in this case it is stuffed fish heads. Eating fish heads is a challenge for most of us I guess, those dead cooked eyes looking up and all that bone to deal with. Yet nutrition experts point out that for example fish cheeks are prime eating and the heads are full of vitamins and minerals. Indeed there are all sorts of fish head dishes around the World. You might not find it on British local Chinese take away menus but if you are in Mainland China a regional fish head dish is bound to appear some where on the menu appealing to bone and cartilage loving patrons. Ranging

throughout South East Asia and including Bangladesh there is a great enthusiasm for fish head curries created with a profusion of different recipes and types of fish. Even in Europe fish heads appeal to some for example Portuguese fish head soup is extremely popular in many quarters. Crappit heid did not start life as a specialty dish but one of necessity. Fishermen, particularly those from the North East Scottish coast and the Islands, removed the heads from the bigger fish in their catch at their customers' requests or to salt or smoke them. What to do with the heads, plenty good protein and fat so not to be wasted therefore pack the head with cheep carbohydrate and you have the basis of a balanced meal? The heads at first were stuffed with oatmeal or barley plus suet and chopped onion also any fish innards that had been removed during preparation. The heads were sewed up and boiled to provide a nutritious, if not entirely pleasant, meal. *"Meg Dods"* in her *"The Cook and Housewife's Manual"* from the 1820s stated that during her time crappit heid went a little up market by being stuffed with egg, anchovy, crab or lobster. I guess Scots preferred their crab and lobster without fish head involvement so thankfully by the 20th and 21st Centuries crappit heid was extinct!

3. **Hattit Kit** - It is a dish incomprehensible to most of us in Scots but also it is intriguing when translated into modern English. Hattit (or hatted) is to be wearing a hat. There is a recipe for hatted kit in *"F Marian McNeill's"* recipe book called *"The Scots Kitchen"* from the 1920s she instructs us that our hatted kit is a milk, cream and

buttermilk concoction. Actually buttermilk contains no butter but it is the tangy and watery by product of the one time traditional means of turning cream into butter. She emphasizes that the milk needs to be as fresh as possible even straight from the cow. "*Catherine Brown*", edited the more recent versions of the *"McNeill"* book, informing us that a kit was a wooden vessel into which all the ingredients are poured. In the kit is where the milk separates out into solid curds on top and clear whey beneath. The solid curds form the covering hat (hattit) while we are told the kit needs a tap or opening low down so that the clear liquid whey can be drained off when required. The hat can be creamed from the top of the kit and it is strained to make it even more solid. In modern times the curds are solidified further in the fridge but when your hatted kit is eaten it is flavoured classically with sugar, nutmeg, sometimes cinnamon and a dribble of double cream. I am not quite sure how far back this old Highland recipe goes but authors were writing about it in the 1600s. *"McNeill"* suggested that the dish was ideal for children and invalids but through out its history, it had a much wider appeal than that being a decent dessert for a wide range of tastes. I have never seen a kit (except in books) and it is not much of an assumption that this is true for most people. On the other hand you can make a decent hattit kit in a pan. Simply warm the buttermilk gently and add milk then leave most of a day until curds form. Strain the curds and flavour as you wish.

4. **Clootie Dumpling** - Dumpling is a strange British word in its own right that on consensus seems to go

back to 17ᵗʰ Century East Anglia although that is by no means certain. There are all sorts of dumplings around the World. Of the two basic styles, one is a solid creation as enjoyed in Britain and Germany whereas the other has a central filling with a cover such as is popular in China and its neighbours. Another way of considering dumplings is on the basis of whether they are sweet or savoury. In these Islands savoury ones are cooked floating in stews to bulk up the dish. Whereas the sweet puddings are exceptionally rich and provide a massive calorie hit. One of those solid but sweet family of desserts is clootie dumpling harking back to a time when the sweet dumpling mixture was wrapped in a cloth (cloot) and steamed or boiled in a large pot by the fire as a big slightly flattened ball of goodness. The pudding batter recipe varies from place to place but usually consists of flour, suet or butter, spices like cinnamon, ginger and nutmeg, baking soda, lots of sugar, dried fruits in abundance, treacle, eggs and milk (often soured). A good glug of whisky into the batter does not go amiss. Then the cook submerges a pudding cloth in water, rings it out and drenches the damp cloth with flour. The batter is placed on the cloth and the edges of the cloth brought together and tied leaving sufficient room inside for expansion of the pudding during cooking. Take a large pot and put a plate on the bottom on which the clootie will rest, then cover with water on the boil. Simmer your pudding for 2 to 3 hours then serve up with custard for a tasty treat. Most Scots have heard of clootie dumpling but sadly few have tried it and even less have made it.

IRELAND

1. **Farl** - strange name don't you think? If you hadn't heard the name before you think it was some tool from a farmyard or an impoverished serf from ancient times perhaps? Now if you were from Ulster or Scotland it would be quite familiar and would be associated either with soda or potato breads. It is my understanding that the Northern Irish word "farl" is derived from the now obsolete Scots word "fardel" meaning a quarter of something circular. In other words it is a quadrant. Soda bread is very popular throughout the whole of Ireland much more so than in England, Wales and Scotland. The three historically preferred yeast-based bread and got it from commercial bakeries. The Irish on the other hand usually baked their bread at home and made soda bread (chemical raising agent) in preference to yeast bread (biological raising agent) because the former was more reliable and easier to cook on a skillet by the fire. In current times you can get any type of bread you want throughout Ireland but soda bread is still seen as being special. Only in the North however is the bread routinely divided into four ("farls"). The other dish is the potato farl made from left over mash, flour, butter

and salt. A flat circle of potato dough is cut into four farls and shallow fried on both sides. Bigger than their Scottish cousin, the "potato scone" goes brilliantly with fried foods particularly eggs and bacon or how about grilled tomatoes with a sprinkling of cheese?

2. **Crubeens** - My Scots Grandpa had Irish blood in him that did not show too much except at Sunday night supper time when crubeens might make an appearance but only if he was in Grannie's good books. Of course crubeens is the Irish name for pigs' trotters and these feet take ages to prepare so on Grannie's part it was very much a labour of love. They were only ever eaten as a late supper because they took hours to cook and quite a lot of preparation and cleaning before hand. She set up a slow cook casserole containing onions, carrots, celery and potatoes around the crubeens plus lots of seasoning. A lump of bacon added additional flavour and a chopped up cabbage was introduced late on during the 3 to 4 hours of cooking. At this point the trotters were falling apart; just how Grandpa liked them. Some cooks like to wrap the crubeens in cloth or some such to keep them together but Grandpa liked his to be disintegrating into the soupy stew. At that point he helped himself to a huge bowl of meat, fat, vegetables and stock. He sat at the kitchen table with a pal to help him out. Not one of us, God no! The slurping and talking to the food was too gross for the family. It was our fat dog who was in her element slurping in harmony with Grandpa - nasty! At one time in Ireland at least crubeens were popular café and pub food. They were served either boiled in

a dish or parboiled, crumb-coated and fried as finger food. Publicans know all too well the salty crubeens went perfectly with a smooth pint of Guinness or two. Tastes change with the generations and these days even in Ireland a plate of crubeens is hard to find even in traditional Irish restaurants. They are in butchers shops and markets so people in some Irish homes still find the time to prepare them.

3. **Goody** - Catholic and Orthodox countries among others celebrate St John's Day on the 24th June. The John is *John the Baptist* who is reputed to have been executed on this day. Celebrations begin on the Eve of the festival with bonfires and a firework display. I remember it as being a big deal in places like Spain where young men jump through the fires with a little goading from their peers. In Ireland they have bonfires also and traditionally back in the day the children and adults enjoy a mug of goody. The dish basically is cubes of stale bread heated up in milk, sugar and spices. These days goody is still made in many homes often as a winter warmer or to ward off illness. My one time mother-in-law Maureen thought it the ultimate medicine. When anyone had the slightest cough or sniffle they would be kindly cajoled into eating a mug of goody. If no cold developed then goody had done its job but if you did get a cold then it would have turned into flu without the mug of goody! I was always a very difficult patient because I can't stand warm milk spiced or otherwise. I would refuse my goody right up to the last moment when I was threatened by the second cold remedy, potcheen (home made whiskey) and raw

egg. Faced with this second horror the milky goody did not seem quite so bad.

4. **Spice Bag** - It sounds like it is something you keep on a rack in the kitchen for adding to exotic meals or as a dish it might come from the Middle East but hardly from Ireland surely? Yet spice bag is a popular Irish dish created in Chinese take away places in Dublin sometime back 10 years or so. If that seems pretty vague it is because the exact origins are obscure and there are several poorly substantiated claims. Yet it has been reported in local newspapers that a more than decent candidate for the origins of spice bag is a Chinese take away place called *"The Sunflower"* in the southwest Dublin suburb of Templeogue. They put together the dish back in and around 2010 and have been selling spice bag ever after. From there, fairly rapidly, more and more Chinese take away places and chippies started to offer spice bags until it became a late night treat through out Dublin. From the capital it spread throughout Ireland in a remarkably short time. Essentially the meal consists of chips/fries in a bag (or now often a box) with fried onions, sliced peppers, chopped chilli and a mixture of spices including Indian cumin, ground coriander, ginger and Chinese five spice. The meat can be pork but usually it is bite-sized lumps of battered fried chicken. If you have had a few beers and fancy eating tasty, salty, fatty, spicy street food then a spice bag is for you. It tastes just great as you wander your way home slightly worse for wear. It never tastes quite the same if you are sitting down and quite sober.

WALES

1. **Crempog** - I have to say it does sound to me like some cleaver device you might need if you we climbing mountains. Perhaps even a complication that sometimes occurs after a near fatal illness perhaps? Well it turns out crempog is just a name for Welsh pancakes, certainly it is the most common one but as it turns out these pancakes have plenty of different names. It just depends on which part of Wales you happen to be eating them. Crempog is the term used specifically in North Wales and the one, rather than the others, that has spread beyond the Welsh borders. This is a leavened pancake that consists of a mixture of flour, butter, yeast (or bicarbonate of soda), an egg, sugar and buttermilk. Invariably, and a characteristic of this type of pancake, there is often the addition to the recipe of a little vinegar that is sufficient to contribute to the background taste. Most crempog are plain but some cooks like to add some dried fruit particularly a scattering of currants. Crempog can be eaten at any time of the day, for example they are nice topped with butter and jam for an afternoon snack. Warm or cold they make a decent night-time supper with cream cheese and fresh fruit. It is, however, as a breakfast regular that crempog are best

enjoyed. Good with bacon and honey but even better just hot with melted butter (at least for my tastes).

2. **Miser's Feast** - Surely a total contradiction of terms since misers don't approve of any of that expensive feasting business do they? All cultures have within their cuisines some sorts of frugal dishes when money is tight so they are economic, reasonably tasty and definitely filling. England has its bubble and squeak made from leftovers, Italy enjoys its bread soup that combines tomato and bread to bulk it out, French cassoulet uses beans and any remnant meat that is at hand while in Spain and Mexico migas is a frugal breakfast of sausage, fried bread and anything to be used up. Actually Welsh miser's feast is quite a tasty dish and a perfectly reasonable family meal. You slice parcooked potatoes thinly using a sharp knife, a processor or a mandolin to produce plenty of potato circles, then do the same with a few white onions. Have plenty butter handy, chopped bacon rashers and beef stock. Have one pork chop per person on the side plus a few sprigs of thyme and plenty salt and pepper. Take a wide casserole dish and grease the base with a little butter, create a layer of potato circles, then some butter, onion and chopped bacon, now more potato and so on so that you end up with a top layer of potato circles. Season, and thyme on top. Make a pork chop topping and pour over the stock. The dish then goes in a hot oven (180⁰C) for around 1 hour. Pork chop is a relatively recent addition to the miser's feast. In times past it would only be bacon and that dish could be cooked on the hob and served with an egg and some greens.

3. **Laverbread** - A laver is a kind of basin for washing and in the Jewish religion a receptacle for special cleansing required in religious ceremonies. It is also a seaweed called *Porphyra umbilicalis* that is edible and found on seashores of parts of Britain. Other edible *Porphyra* species are found the World over and form a significant part of the diet in numerous countries in South East Asia. In Wales however the seaweed is boiled (for many hours), pounded and minced before it is ready to cook. Laver, in the form of "laverbread", has become a National treasure. Once fried, it becomes Welshman's caviar according to the famous actor Richard Burton. So where does the bread part come in? Well it doesn't, the dish is just boiled, bashed and fried seaweed - though sometimes it is served up on fried bread or toast. After all that hard work preparing "laverbread" I have to say it looks like over-cooked black cabbage that has been pummeled by the rim of a saucer like my Mum used to do. It doesn't smell all too cleaver either (at least to me). The seaweed carries that slightly off smell you get when the tide has just gone out. It is "Marmite-like" not in respective tastes but you either love or hate them. Laverbread is often served up with lamb at dinner and also at breakfast with eggs and bacon. Like other edible seaweeds it is rich in antioxidants and fibre while in addition "laverbread" has a massive iodine content.

4. **Oggie** - you may or may not be aware of the great oggie controversy? The "Cornish pasty" and the "Welsh oggie" are both pasties of a similar appearance and composition but which of them came first? Well in

Cornwell there is no controversy at all. Tin miner's wives made them for their husband's lunch starting back in the 17th Century. The wives made a pasty in the morning filling the centre of a pastry circle with coarsely chopped skirt of beef, onion and swede. There after the pastry is folded over and the edges crimped before cooking. The pasty differs from the "Scots bridie" by containing a fair portion of vegetable (that can be of quite variable content), never being made of puff pastry and having a far more pronounced area of crimping. Mythology states that the wives would shout "oggie, oggie, oggie" into the mine and to the response "oi, oi, oi" would drop their pasties down the shaft. Personally I don't believe a word of that - meat pies at the time were far too expensive to throw anywhere especially down some hole in the ground! Seems to me it is wishful thinking the Cornish version came before the Welsh delicacy. The "Welsh oggie", containing leeks as well as the other constituents, was sustenance for labourers for hundreds of years. Indeed, there is evidence that during construction of "St David's Cathedral" in the 12th Century the building workers waded through more than their fair share of "Welsh oggies". If that is the case the Welsh counterpart makes the "Cornish pasty" look like a mere infant.

HOLLAND

1. **Funfair soup** - sounds really odd to me. You have rides at funfairs, sideshows, amusement arcades and eat loads of burgers, popcorn and candy-floss but who in their right mind negotiates a fairground with a plate of chunky broth to hand? Well it seems that the Dutch are partial to soups on these occasions and they appear to be very keen on a meat plus meatball concoction that also contains celery, spinach, sorrel leaves, asparagus and noodles. For once here we have a dish where the name avoids being misleading, it is no way euphemistic, nor is it at all gruesome. In fact, quite unusual for this book, the name of this hot dish is in line with what it is - a soup to be enjoyed at funfairs or on special celebrations (as simple as that). "Meatballs" of all shapes and sizes, with or without "noodles", are highly regarded in Holland so they are constituents of numerous dishes. The big boys (Dutch "meatballs" can be rather large) star as part of a substantial dinner while smaller versions can be found stacked up as a tasty a bar snack. Back however to our "funfair soup" and those special Dutch annual funfairs (in Dutch called "kermis"), events that are often massive especially in the South. Take the Tilberg Funfair as an

example which goes on for 10 days and the attractions including parades, theatre, music venues, market stalls and rides that are spread over a stretch of nearly 3 miles. I guess you would need a bowl of nutritious "funfair soup" after all that. I still find it hard to imagine eating "meatballs, noodles and broth" on top of the big wheel ride, the wall of death or the dodgems for that matter! Mind you in my time I have done all of those with a face covered in "candy floss".

2. **Hot Lightning** - it sounds like it should be a fierce and fiery dish! In Holland there are exceptional Indonesian restaurants with some hot and not so hot but always delicious meals. However this dish is not to be found on an exotic South East Asian menu. In fact it is fairly ordinary in composition although delightful non-the-less. "Hot lightning" is a filling plate of potatoes, chopped onion and sweet and sour apples or even pears in a mash. The ratio of apple to potato is variable but should not be less than 1 apple to two potatoes going up to parity in some recipes. All are merged together to make a highly satisfying and tasty combination. In terms of Europe, the Dutch were late to take to the potato, only starting to grow them towards the end of the 18th Century. Classically the potato and apple special goes well with "black pudding", a popular Dutch winter warmer. Although I have heard that in some regions of Holland the apple/potato combination is occasionally paired with "meat stew". Whereas in the Brabant, "smoked sausage" is preferred to "black pudding" but only in some places. Overall throughout Holland, it

is "black pudding" that is the typical partner for "hot lightening" (known locally as "hete bliksem") to the extent that "black pudding" is often considered the final constituent of the dish. Why name it "hot lightening"? A reasonable explanation is that the apple helps retain the cooking heat in the mixture far more readily than potato alone so you can easily burn your mouth as I have found to my cost. The name "hot lightening" is not exclusive as it is also called by some Dutch "Heaven and Earth" ("Hemel en Aarde"). As it turns out, much the same meal is enjoyed in many parts of Germany where also it is also referred to as "Heaven and Earth" in their language. Presumably an apple hanging from a tree is Heaven and the potato growing in soil is Earth?

3. **Five Breaks** - like "hot lightening", "five breaks" is also an apple-rich dish. It is a "hotpot" of apples and vegetables, particularly carrots, while the meat is fine-chopped "smoked bacon". In addition "five breaks" has plenty of dried beans, rehydrated overnight before being added to the pot. It seems back in the 19th Century a love sick young Dutchman, presumably short of sufficient funds to keep the prospective wife in the style she was accustomed, declared to his sweetheart that if she would be his, he would work "five breaks" each day. It seems the normal working arrangement in Holland at that time involved four breaks. So I guess a five-break day would require working more hours and so result in a higher wages. There is no obvious connection between our dish and the hardworking guy except "five breaks" with its combination of bacon, beans, fruit and

vegetables is suitably nutritious for someone working long hours. "Hotpot" dishes of the "five breaks" type are much loved in Holland as winter warmers and this one originated in Utrecht. The City is right in the middle of Holland and famed for its churches, picturesque canals, old university and the place where Kaiser Wilhelm II lived out his days following defeat in WWI! "Five breaks" is not a very well known Dutch meal possibly because the meat component is "smoked bacon". Bacon is mostly not smoked in Holland for that matter smoked meat and fish is less appreciated there than in other European countries although the Dutch do like their "smoked sausage" ("rookworst"), "smoked eel" is a delicacy ("gerookte paling") and of course "smoked cheeses" abound ("gerookte kaas").

BELGIUM

1. **Boiled Water** - sounds like a very weak soup indeed but soup is exactly what it is. I've slurped my way through some pretty watery soups in my time but this is not one because it is so thick some call it a stew. Our soup, called "waterzooi", is known and appreciated throughout Belgium although it is at its best and most popular in Ghent were "boiled water" soup originates. The original recipes show it to be fish and seafood based. A range of vegetables with plenty of potatoes is essential. Chunks of white fish, mussels and the local brown shrimp make up the bulk of the dish and it is all set off with good stock. So originally a fish soup/stew it has in more recent times morphed into a thick chicken soup. These days a chopped up whole chicken has replaced the fish and seafood component in most recipes. Some places stick to the old ways but for the most part if you ask for "waterzooi" in Belgium it is a substantial chicken stew for you to mop up with copious amounts of fresh bread. Ghent is a beautiful and ancient city, crisscrossed with numerous canals. Back in the day the canals were the major source of the "waterzooi" fish component. I've been up and down these canals many times in my life

having first holidayed in Ghent when I was fourteen. The waterways are much cleaner now but you don't need to go back too far into the past to appreciate why there was the fish to chicken change over. However whether you eat this thick soup with a chicken, fish or seafood base it is exquisite but "boiled water" has to be a totally crazy name!

2. **Birds' Nests** - a well-known Chinese dish is "bird's nest soup" made out of the glue that holds a swift's nest together. I've never eaten the dish but from the pictures I've seen, it doesn't look all that appetizing. Mind you it would be hard to make bird's gluey spit look good in any circumstance! On the other hand the Belgian "bird's nest" is entirely different from the Chinese version. Essentially the dish consists of a hard-boiled egg, surrounded by a combination of seasoned beef and pork mince. The egg and its meat covering is coated with breadcrumbs and deep-fried. Yes, it does seem familiar - it is the Belgian meatball version of the famous "Scotch egg"! They are called "vogelnestje" in the Flemish part of Belgium where "bird's nest meatballs" originate. These Belgian "birds nests" are eaten sparingly throughout the year but particularly they are associated with Easter celebrations. At this time the "bird's nest meatballs" share a plate with pink mashed potatoes (just normal mash with plenty milk and a lot of tomato puree) and a lake of rich tomato sauce. As you might imagine, children love this Easter meal and look forward to it. When they cut their mince covered boiled egg in half, it requires only a little imagination to see them as two

nests with egg inside. Coated hard-boiled eggs like the ubiquitous "Scotch egg" and the much lesser known "vogelnestje" are not uncommon around the World. For example in Northern India there is "nargisi kofta" a boiled egg surrounded with "kema" and cooked in curry sauce whereas in South America a "cassava mash" is a common covering for a boiled egg-based street food. In Japan it is common to "tempura coat" and deep fry boiled eggs while fried breadcrumb-coated boiled eggs are enjoyed in many countries.

3. **Blind Finches** - in times not too long ago, songbird eating was Europe-wide. These days it still goes on occasionally in Italy but fortunately it no longer is the festivity it once was. There is still an issue in France and other places including some Balkan countries and the Mediterranean island of Cyprus even although there are explicit European regulations banning songbird hunting and eating. It's a long time since rich Belgians enjoyed a plate of cooked finches but when they did it was fine dining and not for the poor workers. Their wives came up with a "mock lark" dish consisting of a strip of sirloin bashed flat as possible. The stuffing consists of savoury mince mixed with egg, breadcrumbs and chopped onion. As with other meat stuffings, meatballs and even burgers, it is good to add some breadcrumbs to act as binding but also they help keep the cooked mixture moist (as the meat cooks the juices are trapped in the crumbs keeping the whole thing juicy). The filling is wrapped in the flattened meat to make a parcel and tied with string. The parcels look vaguely bird like but there

are no eyes - so "blind finches" or as they are known in the north "vogeltjes zonder kop". In modern Belgium, finch dinners are not to be had thankfully but trays of "blind finches" are on display in every Belgian butcher's shop just as "beef olives" are on sale in all Scots butchers. Indeed thin strips of meat wrapped over a stuffing can be found in the cuisines of many countries. For example "beef braciola" is a Southern Italian winter staple consisting of thin beef strips surrounding a savoury stuffing served in a rich tomato sauce. Later on (under France) there is a description of "headless larks" another beef covered savoury dish. In South East Asia "beef rollups" contain numerous vegetables and are cooked in soy sauce.

4. **American Fillet** (filet Americain) - now that sounds delicious! Surely we are talking about a tender fillet steak, some Belgian fries (the country is the home of chips after all) and a nice sauce - yummy. I have to say that our Belgian, "American fillet" does contain beef but it is the minced up, raw kind so enjoyed by gourmets in France. The Belgian "steak tartare" (either fillet or sirloin steak) contains a bunch of things you would find in this dish elsewhere such as chopped onion, raw egg, capers, chopped cornichons, Tabasco, Worcestershire sauce etc. In addition there are distinctively Belgian options such as mayonnaise, mustards and other items. Here in Belgium, "American fillet" has no snob value whatsoever and most general butchers supply the dish often prepared fresh on request by the customer. In cafes and the like the raw beef mince is sometimes served as a

round on a square of dry toast along with salad reveling in the gruesome name of "toast kannibaal." In addition, a very Belgian treat, found everywhere in that country, is their "tartare" preparation used as a sandwich filling for a "baguette roll". The snack is known locally as a "martino". I have to say, as a "steak tartar" lover, the "martino" drops the dish a class or so. No bad thing some might say? I'm not so sure but those around me say I have foodie pretentions that defy logic. After all French "steak tartar" is to all intents and purposes an uncooked "burger" without the bun but many times more expensive. Finally why call the Belgian version of French "steak tartare" a "filet Americain"? Well it is a joke although perhaps more of a dig at different food culture values. Seemingly American troops during the War were horrified when they saw Belgians enthusiastically eating minced raw meat!

FRANCE

1. **Financier** - I suppose a financier is a person who manipulates money on behalf of small and large organizations. One such person in the City of London described himself as taking money from the cash rich and supplying it to those who require it but at a price! The same breed of people inhabits all the financial capitals of the world including Paris. In this city the business and financial hub is located around the Bourse (stock exchange) on the right bank of the River Seine However in Paris there is a second "financier" and that is a small individual and usually rectangular sponge cake. The French name is "visitandine" describing both the movers and shakers around the Bourse and our local cake. Surprisingly for a French fancy, it is rather on the plane side but on the other hand our cake has a delicious almond and "beurre noisette" ("nutty butter") taste. The story goes that the simple cake was a 19th Century creation made first by a Paris chef who supplied cakes to clients in Paris' financial district where he had established his restaurant. Our baker created his almond butter-rich cakes believing they would appeal to white-collar workers in the nearby offices by not

being messy. He was correct, these people could not get enough of this new treat that was tasty but did not stain fingers or cuffs. Since the little golden cakes were made in rectangular molds, they reminded the office workers of mini gold bars. As a result "financier" seemed an entirely appropriate name.

2. **Headless Larks** - it sounds like a pretty disgusting dish by any ecological standard! I understand from newspaper articles that Frenchmen armed to the teeth, thinking themselves brave hunters, slaughter little songbirds without remorse. It is still going on with an unbelievable annual kill that has been estimated to be in the region of 17 million birds per year. In French cuisine, there are numerous songbird recipes but most of these harmless creatures are not destined for the pot only for the bin in the name of "sport". The lark sings as it flies and filled the countryside with melody. Sadly this much loved songbird numbers are in sharp decline in many countries so definitely it doesn't need to be hunted the lark has problems enough. With my rant out of the way, I need to point out that no French sportsman or cook has decapitated larks to make this dish. The name is a classic miss direction not at all uncommon in naming dishes around the World. In Belgium we had our "blind finches" (see earlier) and in the same vein "headless larks", or "alouettes sans tetes", are not at all what they first appear to be. It is a Provencal dish consisting of parcels of beef filled with pork, vegetables and herbs cooked in a rich garlicy tomato sauce. Excellent in all but the name and similar

in many ways to the Italian "beef braciola" but with a much nastier name.

3. **Grandma Rum** - you probably think this is a French food that has passed you by but in French the name is "Baba au Rhum" and in English "Rum Baba". The old school "Rum Baba," is rarely seen in UK bakeries these days but still remain popular in parts of France where the cake originated. It is a sponge cake baked in a ring mold and the batter mix is filled with raisins soaked in rum. Once cooked, more rum is added to the cake and the centre is filled with whipped cream, pastry cream or some such delight. Smaller versions of the "rum baba" exist such as a finger cake with a zigzag squirt of whipped cream on top. The cake was the invention of a 19th Century pastry chef called Nicolas Stohrer who worked for Queen Marie Leszcyznska wife of King Louis XV. He created his specialty in honour of the exiled "King Stanislas" of Poland his patron's father. The original cake was created when Stohrer was in the Royal kitchens in Poland and was moistened with East European wine and embellished with a type of custard. The transformation involving rum and additional whipped cream presumably occurred in Paris where in 1730 chef Stohrer opened a cake shop. His pastries and the "ruhm au baba" were a great success with the locals. In the Slavic language Baba is grandma or old woman but why the delicious, over the top, cake should be named "grannies rum" defeats me but does make for an even more curious name for our confection. Another possibly more credible alternative explanation is that

King Stanislas, who was now in exile in Paris, admired Arabian stories so the "Baba" cake name is more likely the hero of "Ali Baba and the 40 Thieves". Indeed you still can buy the cakes from the Stohrer shop in Paris and of the "Babas" their largest circular version with old school custard has the title "the original Ali Baba" so it is clear from the Stohrer patisserie whom the cake was named after. In addition I suspect King Stanislas knew that in Arabic "alibaba" sort of translates to "top leader."

4. **Crunch in the Mouth** - such a very French dessert, only to be made and constructed by the talented, patient or insane pastry cook. It translates to "croque en bouche" or in recipe books as "croquembouche". Personally I think this construction should be "heart in the mouth" rather than "crunch in the mouth". I love to cook but never have been tempted to construct the gravity-defying "croquembouche". It was one of the many culinary masterpieces created by the unique Antonine Careme back in the 18th Century. He was the very first celebrity chef who you might call upon if you had a wedding dinner, celebration meal or banquet to organise but only if you were famous, mega rich, royalty or preferably all three. For example I read that the Baron de Rothschild had Careme on an annual retainer equivalent to £125,000 for his very occasional services. What did all these rich folks get for their considerable investment? Well he was the greatest chef of his time (or arguably of any time), a consummate showman who had the skill and imagination to create the ultimate dining experience that had "a wow factor"

plus much more. Beyond the celebrity bit, he was a true innovator and set the stage for the development of modern French cuisine. The "croquembouche" is all about building food castles in the sky with a Careme basic unit, the spherical profiterole made from choux pastry and filled with cream or custard. If you are Careme, a decent pastry chef or you have a degree in geometry any cook can build a "croquembouche" tower of any shape. However the classic configuration is an inverted cone and the glue is melted toffee or chocolate painted on the outside of each profiterole. Once set, the edifice is reasonably stable; at least until the temperature goes up or some hungry people want dessert.

SWITZERLAND

1. **Backpacker** - one of the many on line definitions of a backpacker is "a person who travels or hikes carrying their belongings in a rucksack". Now I've done a bit of travelling in my time, as a kid I went across Europe with other teenagers. As I remember, it involved a lot of sleeping in barns and only occasional washing. Also I crossed America in an old Jeep that never managed to get above 50 miles an hour. There were a ridiculous number of stop-overs in cheep motels with friendly cockroaches and nasty "pizzas". My son Matthew on the other hand had has had the proper tee shirt or more correctly rucksack lifestyle travelling the World for years. I never knew what part of the planet he would be in next. Now when it comes to Switzerland, I have found that place is full of backpackers in one form or another. Mostly not the real backpackers who are too busy abseiling in the Andes or canoeing down rapids in North Island New Zealand. No there is a designer backpacker who has reached more elderly years and has a coach to follow his or her wanderings up mountain trails and around scenic lakes that this country has to offer in abundance. The bus supplies rest, chilled

wine, canopies and encouragement when their aging backpackers start to falter. "Landjager" translates as "land hunter" is not really for them even although its nickname is "backpacker". After all it is just a very Swiss dry, beef and pork, spicy sausage that keeps forever in a backpack. Ideal for the high mountain hiking, jet skiing, micro lite brigade or even hunters and soldiers but not for the connoisseur with a bus full of hors d'oeuvres and fine wines at the ready. "Landjager" is good food for tough guys and perhaps not quite so tough guys. I can tell you from experience that in the Swiss Alps during January the hot (or cold) sausage goes well with bread and potatoes plus loads of hot "gluwein" on the side. Invigorating food for the hardy backpackers and hunters prior to their hike up the mountains. For my part I'm staying put indoors by the fire, bloody cold out there! I wonder when the designer coach is coming? Hope they have the heating on and lots of treats!

2. **Cholera** - you have to shudder once or twice at the thought of eating a nice plate of cholera. The disease is caused by ingestion of the infective bacteria from infected food or water. Sufferers, without treatment, can die of diarrhoea and dehydration frighteningly quickly. In this time of pandemics (written 2022) I am reminded of the numerous cholera pandemics in the past (and the remarkably recent past) that have infected millions. Back in 1836 there was a cholera outbreak in central Europe that was particularly ferocious in Switzerland. As we know only too well, when disease is rampant one sensible thing is to stay at home so Switzerland

had a massive lockdown. In those times there were no supermarkets to help out so people had to fall back on their own resources. What they had in their home store cupboard, what was in the garden or what they could shoot or forage was all they had available. Creative menus and considerable ingenuity was required to keep families fed. In the canton of Valais to the south west of Switzerland, is Goms. In that town they created a simple savoury pie later named rather perversely "Gomser cholera". The recipe has been adapted over the two centuries of its existence but essentially it is a puff pastry pie filled with layers starting with chopped onion, leek, apple and bacon mix, then sliced potato, followed by the famous "raclette cheese". After that repeat the layers and top with pastry then cook in the oven and you have a tasty pie. The pie is made from whatever is at hand in the garden and available on the shelves of the store cupboard in keeping with "make do" origins of the dish. Despite the grim name "Cholera" is pleasantly filling. It is in keeping with the vegetable short crust pie, created in England during WWII, and called "Woolton pie" after Lord Woolton the wartime minister of food. Both are products of ingenuity during times of adversity. Hopefully cholera pandemics are a thing of the past but a sobering thought is that between 1 and 4 million people get the disease every year.

3. **Salted Sugar** - now I have a book at home that talks about what goes with what and also what really doesn't sit side by side on a plate. I get what some of the book says but it looses me too often. There is a whole section

that goes on about salty foods off set by sweetness - well not sure about that. Clearly I don't have sophisticated taste buds. Each of our taste buds distinguishes sweet, salty, sour, bitter and umami (savoury) but although I like sweet and salty individually, in many instances, I dislike them together. "Chocolate pretzels" are nasty and I cannot get the "salted caramel" thing at all!. My daughter Megan, when restaurants are open and we have less restricted access, loves me to order for her American-style pancakes topped with salty, streaky bacon and dripping in maple syrup and blueberries. How can anyone with a normal set of taste buds take a bite of such a monstrosity! She loves this dish any time of day and I look on in horror (dads and daughters thing I guess). In the Western French part of Switzerland, more specifically the canton of Vaud, they are known for their delicious flat cream cakes. The base is not so much cake as pizza dough but topped with thick sugary whipped cream often flavoured with cinnamon. These "cream rounds" sound not at all bad but one version "salee sucree", which translates as "salted sugar" is the "cream round" topped by bacon bits! Megan would love that monstrosity. It makes me ill just to view the basic recipe.

ITALY

1. **Priest choker** - in Italy, in the past and even today, the pastoral role of the local priest is a key part of their broader duties to the community. The priest visits local families in their homes to get to know them all outside the church environment and its rituals. If a meal was on offer then so much the better. It was, particularly in rural areas where the priest might have to travel quite far, conventional despite family finances to serve up a decent meal to your visitor. Despite the dictates of hospitality, for poor families an extra, rather indulgent, mouth at dinner could be a real burden. The story goes that it was common to serve up a generous portion of "strozzapreti" (or what we are calling "priest choker") early on as the pasta course. The "priest choker" is a thick stringy rustic pasta intended to pack empty bellies rather than to look good. The intention with their clerical guest was to fill up the priest sufficiently with cheap fare so he would be less of a glutton when the more expensive meat courses were presented. "Strozzapreti" is associated with several regions of Italy but none more so than the Papal States. Here in times past, particularly in the last years before their ending in the 19th Century, the priesthood

in the main were really crappy politicians, hopeless administration and wedded to religious conservatism. Not a nice combination so the population really wished the "priest choker" did its work to the letter and as often as possible. In modern day Italy "strozzapreti" is a more than decent pasta creation, with a bit of a checkered past, that goes extremely well with rich tomato sauce and a whole range of seafood combinations.

2. **White Mountain** - English is a very functional language, spoken by many people on this planet but it doesn't have much of a "ring" to it - just lacks any presence. A favourite fish in Spain is "merluza", sounds great but in English it is "hake" and not so popular. The French enjoy "crème brulee" as a special treat but in Britain it was originally known as "burnt cream". While the great Italian composer "Giuseppe Verdi" if he were British would simply be "Joe Green". With this in mind, "white mountain" becomes ridiculously more attractive "Mont Blanc" in French and "Monte Bianco" in Italian. It is a mountain and range shared between the two countries. It is the largest peak in the Alps. Although in kitchens and restaurants throughout Northern Italy, it is also a luxurious dessert. Basically it consists of chestnuts cooked in vanilla and milk then pureed. The puree has added sugar and rum. You pour the chestnut mix into a bowl and chill it until solid. Whip up your cream and add even more sugar. Remove the chestnut from the bowl and you have a mountain, coat it with whipped cream and you have your "white mountain" ("Monte Bianco"). All it needs is some decoration such as a

scattering of bottled cherries, white chocolate buttons, meringue, cream swirls, silver balls, glitter and all sorts of mountainous treats.

3. **Music Paper** - this is gossamer thin bread that it is so thin and transparent you can read "carta di musica" through the dough (in English it translates as music paper). The bread is made from 00 flour, semolina, water and salt and after kneading the dough, and cutting it into discs, the bread product is often run through a pasta machine to get it to that necessary thinness. Traditionally however the dough is flattened with a heavy rolling pin by a chef with plenty of skill and patience. After baking for only a few minutes, they will puff up like many flatbreads from around the World. Out of the oven "carta di musica" is very crisp. You can make them at home if you wish but they are sold fresh in many Italian bakeries and delis. "Carta di musica" are a regional specialty that originated in the Mediterranean island of Sardinia. These flatbreads are absolutely great to eat with a scattering of chopped fresh herbs and a liberal spread of salt. I've been to Sardinia three or four times over the years and "carta di musica" are often there on the table of many dinner-time restaurants for you to enjoy before, with or even after your meal. Imagine you are far from the shops then an abundant supply of "music papers" in your store cupboard is a good idea because the flatbreads don't take up much space and they last forever in a dry place. It was their lightness and longevity that sealed their popularity. Shepherds would take stacks of "music

papers" into the hills and along side abundant wild herbs and strong cheese they always had a tasty meal at hand. I remember my family and I rented a house in the wooded hills of North West Sardinia. We all trekked down to the village for supplies. Being on foot everyone had to carry shopping. My youngest children got to cart back the "carta di musica" because they were so light. Great in principle but we dined on "music paper" crumbs that evening.

4. **Jump in the Mouth** - all right then, I believe most Italian dishes seem to "jump into the mouth" or, at the very least when they are in front of me, they don't seem to last all that long on the plate! With respect to Italian cuisine, when Brits go to Italian restaurants we tend to focus on the pasta and pizza options rather than other alternatives. This is a shame - there are real classic dishes such as creamy "risottos", tasty "bricked chicken" ("pollo al mattone"), excellent "lamb skewers" ("arrosticini"), good steaks ("bistecca") and those veal dishes such as "veal shanks" ("osso bucco") and "jump in the mouth" (the translation of "saltimbocca"). In the UK in particular there is a dislike for eating veal not shared by most of Europe, More to do with the rearing (that can be considered cruel) rather than the eating. Readily available rose, rather than white, veal overcomes the rearing issues to a large extent and pork escalope or flattened chicken breast is a decent substitute for veal I find. Take your meat and flatten it with a rolling pin, place sage leaves on either side and fix them in place with 2 or 3 rashers of "prosciutto". Fry up the meat till the

"prosciutto" is crispy, 2 or 3 minutes per side. Remove your meat and rest it, add butter to the empty pan and then white wine to make a thin sauce. Serve with matchstick fries and some seasoned sliced tomato or just on a bed of greens like spinach. Your "saltimbocca" should then "jump in the mouth" hopefully your own mouth helped along by a glass of white (Gavi) or red (Chianti). "Saltimbocca" pops up as a dish all over Italy but it is most common in the capital city as "saltimbocca alla Romana". However it is not Roman but originated further north in Brescia, although you can't convince Romans of that.

SPAIN

1. **Nuns' Sighs** - they are small cream puffs that have been around in Spain forever as "suspiros de monja". Back in the late Middle Ages, they were made everywhere but were most associated with the bakeries and the kitchens of convents hence the link with nuns. Spain at the time was a divided country Christian kingdoms to the north, Moorish ones to the south. Gradually the Christians prevailed and Spain became one country with an even greater religious fervor than before. As a result hosts of churches, monasteries, convents and cloistered communities were established to glorify God. Once enclosed their cloistered convents the nuns and novices didn't get out much spending their time in prayer, singing, reading religious texts and that sort of thing. Fasts were a way of life but nun's food on non-fast days was far from being basic. Those nuns who took full vows were often from rich families and had tastes to match. The convents were well off, the families and rents saw to that, so meals if not opulent were of good quality and decently prepared. The veiled nuns were neither cooks nor bakers this was a task done by some of the lay nuns and women that made up the convent

community. These skilled kitchen personnel became famous throughout Spain particularly for their sweet baked goods and desserts. The irony being that sugary treats were a legacy from the ousted Moors. The nun's sighs are of the family of bakes created in the convent environment. They are simple little mounds of sweet batter fried so they are crisp on the outside and then given a sugar powder coating. Often they are eaten topped with the crystallized fruits popular throughout Spain. The Spanish took their convent system to the Americas so sweet fritters, including "nuns' sighs", soon followed. The apocryphal story about the nuns who ate these tasty tit bits is that they sighed with delight. A more earthy story goes that eating too many creates a windy tummy so the puffs had a much less polite name than sighs! Rows of greedy, farting Spanish nuns is not really the image you want in your head when eating your "nuns' sigh".

2. **Rotten Pot** - it has got to be one of the great names for a dish don't you think? Especially if you are determined that no one should eat it. Can you imagine a café owner advertising out front on the menu board that there is a really delicious "rotten pot" for lunch? On the other hand I have to say "rotten pot" is a more than decent, usually home-cooked stew perfectly fit to feed the whole family and keep the winter chill at bay. Clearly it is not a restaurant classic by any stretch of the imagination. In fact I've never seen it on any restaurant menu posh or otherwise. "Rotten pot" ("olla podrida") also has a rather special place

it likes to call home and that is Burgos in the north. The dish is also well known in the Spanish capital city of Madrid. You might ask why on Earth would you need comfortable warming food in in a hot place like Madrid? Well as a tourist in summer you would be perfectly correct although if you have been there in December or January you will know that it does get cold - not excessively cold but cold enough if you are used to hot weather. In fact I've known it to snow in Central Spain but only on occasion. In cold weather you retire to your house or apartment that is wonderfully designed to keep heat out but certainly not to keep it in. If you tread bare feet on a tiled floor with the temperature down at about 5^0C, believe me it feels like your walking towards the North Pole dressed only in in your Y-fronts. This is when a big bowl of "olla podrida" comes into its own. The stew varies considerably from place to place but I remember it as being basically a thick broth rich in onions, red peppers, carrots, haricot beans, cheap cuts of pork and spicy sausage. The basic recipe provides a warming meal on a (relatively) cold day in Spain but by adding additionals such as beef shin, chicken drumsticks, black pudding, chickpeas, cabbage and even apple you have an economic winter feast.

3. **Moors and Christians** - not politically correct at all but Moors versus Christian festivals have been part of Southern Spanish social customs for hundreds of years. There is a lot of dressing up either as Christian knights on horseback and their foot soldiers with wicked

looking pikes or Moors with pointy helmets, round shields and big curved swords. One group is in white and red while the other in black or blue and gold parade around shouting abuse at each other. At focal points there are masses of stalls selling everything from food to trinkets so everyone has a good time. The festivals celebrate the Spanish Christian victories over the Moors, which lead to the formation of a unified Kingdom of Spain. Of particular significance to all revelers was the capture of Granada by King Ferdinand and Queen Isabella in 1492 - the main re-enactment (though very loosely) at many of these events. The food stalls have masses of Spanish and Moroccan classics ranging from "paella" to "tagine" dishes. Of course you usually can find somewhere that will sell you a plate of "Moors and Christians" though the dish is somewhat bland, compared to the wide range of delicacies available on the majority of stalls, it is extremely good. There is plenty of boiled white rice (Christians) mixed with even more dark lentils (Moors) and flavoured with olive oil, onions and garlic in a plate of "Moros y Cristianos". The dish is usually garnished with slices of boiled egg and toasted almonds in the North African style. The dish crossed the Atlantic particularly to Cuba and then subsequently elsewhere in the Americas. In Cuba it was, and still is, basically a rice dish although the lentils were replaced by locally grown black beans. In America "Moors and Christians" is considered a Cuban dish but it is an old World creation rather than new World one. Spain cannot take all the credit however because you can get this lentil and rice dish all around the Middle

East and North Africa. Lentils or beans, which is best? As it happens they both are delicious.

4. **A Fish Operetta** - I am not an opera buff and much prefer operettas since they are lighter, usually happier, much shorter and often they are sung in English. I know they are out of vogue and espouse too many Victorian values but I've been a sucker for "Gilbert and Sullivan" all my life. Thus I was delighted one time in "Barcelona" to be told of a rather special Catalan dish has a name that roughly translates to "operetta of fish" ("zarzuela de pescado"). Except of course "zarzuelas" are spectacular musical theatre as Spanish as "Gilbert and Sullivan" is English. The "zarzuelas" are a little over the top and based around a vast array of characters. So it is that "zarzuela de pescado" contains a host of different fish and seafood all immersed in a colourful stock. When in Catalonia I had to try it and to my delight it turned out to be sensational. I am told that the fish can be any combination of white fish that appeals to you (hake, cod and the like) paired with a monkfish tail cut into chunks. Whereas the seafood component includes prawns, mussels, clams, squid rings and lobster. Quite a lot of brandy is introduced taking the flavouring to another level and the vegetables are a classic tomato, garlic, pepper and onion combination forming a tarditional but rich "sofrito". Thereafter a "picada" of bread, almonds and garlic is whizzed up in a processor and added a few minutes before the end of cooking as a tasty thickener. Not a midweek home cook meal I admit but definitely a celebration of Catalan

seafood and cooking. Without any doubt it is a "fish operetta" albeit an extremely rich and expensive one that outclasses the very best Marseilles "bouillabaisse". As an aside "zarzuela" originated in the palace of that name in Madrid, as a result the stew may be Catalan but the type of "operetta" belongs to Spain's capital.

PORTUGAL

1. **Old Clothes** - my Mum, normally a great cook, used to make a Thursday "special omelette" now and then when the fridge had almost empty shelves. Little bowls of the week's leftovers made up the bulk of what was left in there. They were fated to end up in an egg mix. Omelettes are great - this version never was. My point is that the World of leftover dishes, they can be terrible however they also can be fabulous such as "bubble and squeak", "fried rice" from China or "ribollita" an Italian recook classic and many more. Our "old clothes" dish may be less well known than the others (by me at least) but it is as tasty as any of the World's great leftover specials. Mention to a Portuguese, especially one from Lisbon and the north of the country, what do they think of "roupa velha"? The reaction is usually one of delight but the recipe they love varies from region to region and even differs from household to household. I guess, a definition of a leftover meal, is that the constituents need to be flexible. "roupa velha" can be made anytime but it is associated mostly with Christmas. Take the left over salt cod ("bacalhau") and fresh white fish from a previous meal then chopped up leftover cooked

potatoes, cooked greens, onions and garlic and mix them all together. Fry in oil and a little vinegar then pour in egg mixture, break it all up into a hash and you have your meal. There need not be fish, eggs are optional and so on. The dish has travelled but morphed dramatically - for example it is a chopped steak dish in far away Cuba.

2. **Cow's Hand** - according to the Portuguese at least, cows have hands ("mao de vaca"). In this case obviously the handy cow donates a foot to the dish. The cleaned heel is boiled then added to a stew of wine, vegetables, tomato paste, herbs and piri piri sauce to add some bite. Fried sausage and bacon are added to the mix. Thereafter all are cooked until the cow's foot begins to disintegrate. Take the foot out and give it a "hand" to break apart (bad joke sorry). Once back in the stew cook for a while and add the last component, which is tinned (or already cooked) chickpeas. Indeed the full literal Portuguese name for the dish is "mao (hand) "de vaca" (of cow) "com grao" (with chickpeas)". The meaty, fiery chickpea stew is served usually along side a scoop of boiled white rice. The ingredients of that same dish are seen in parts of South America and also Jamaica. They tend, at least from the recipes I've seen, to be more soupy and less spicy than the Portuguese parent dish. In Britain these days dishes based on boiling cows trotters are no longer on our menus (see Ireland and crubeens). Although looking through Victorian recipe books like Eliza Acton and Mrs Beeton, at that time calves or cows trotters, either boiled or fried, were common economy

meals. Indeed my childhood comic hero, "Desperate Dan" from the "Beano" was forever wading his way through "cowheel pie" though in modern times he has to be content merely with "cow pie".

3. **Little Frenchie** - I used to do a week of teaching in the very beautiful city of Porto once a year and also went their for city breaks. As a result I became very familiar with the place. I know its river the Douro with the barges laden with port, I'm familiar with the red-roofed houses and steep streets climbing ever upwards but also I admit to seeking out "little Frenchie" much too often when I'm there. No she is not a lady of the night, a local friend nor even a fellow lecturer - "Francesinha" is a sandwich. Mind you there is nothing little about this sandwich and usually you get a shovel full of chips on the side for good measure. It is the Porto version of the French "croque madame" i.e. a cheese toastie with an egg on top. Now the Portuguese copy is a belly-busting beast of a thing - a lunch time special of humongous proportions. The "little Frenchie" differs depending on your preferred cafe. However for a few Euros you get on your toast, layers of sliced pork, sausage, bacon and in some places even steak. There is cheese of course, the obligatory fried egg and with the toast lid on top the whole skyscraper is warmed up and finally a thick tomato and beer sauce is splurged all over. This is serious eating, not for the diet conscious and I have not yet managed to finish one, never mind cope with the mountain of chips on the side. I believe it was created in the 1970s after the fall of the nasty Salazar

dictatorship and the return of liberal Portuguese exiles from Paris. They missed their French food treats and tried to recreate them Portuguese style. Mind you the anorexic "croque madame" is as close to a "Francesinha" as a mouse is to an elephant!

4. **Camel Drool** - yes I can confirm from personal experience the camel does drool copious amounts of wet, slimy, bubbly stuff. Hard to imagine that this animal is renowned for its ability to conserve water in the desert. To add to their appeal the beasts belch loudly and have really gruesome halitosis. You have to be an ardent camel lover to get up close and personal. I tried it, got the tee shirt but it was badly gobbed on so straight in the bin. Fortunately the dish does not involve actual spittle, camel or otherwise. It is a much-loved children's (and adult's) pudding, which in Portuguese is called "baba de camilo". There are only four main ingredients that includes a big tin of "dulce de leche" (you can make your own from a of sweetened condensed milk under boiling water but it's a faff), egg yolks, egg whites and on top a sprinkle of nuts or something sweet The "dulce de leche" is mixed with the egg yolks until even, then whisked egg white folded in with the minimum of fuss and poured into dessert glasses. Place in the fridge until the pudding firms up and at the last minute (just before serving) sprinkle something on top. Plenty of almond flakes are traditional but grated chocolate is good and crushed biscuit is quite popular. There are camels in Portugal used in the south for tourist rides

and the like but the most famous camel in the Algarve at least is "praia do camilo" or camel beach. A small crowed double beach at the very south of Portugal but very spectacular and fortunately this beach does not "drool" - except of course at a stormy high tide when it is called foam!

RUSSIA AND UKRAINE

1. **Settler's Soup** - Russia and the Ukraine may have their political issues these days but they have much in common, including cuisines that spectacularly overlap. One dish happily nestled in the overlap is "settler's soup", born probably in the Ukraine back in the 17th Century it is as much loved in Russia as it is in its possible country of origin. In reality we are talking not about one soup but three in all. "Solyanka" at it's most robust contains meats like beef, sausage, ham, chicken or a combination of some or all of them. There is also a fish version usually consisting of a combination of salmon and crayfish while the vegetarian options are dominated by combinations of different types of mushroom. The soups have an interesting vegetable content, pickle and spice combinations but they are essentially sweet and sour. Usually there is plenty chopped cabbage, some sliced potato, olives, tomatoes, salted cucumber (plus the brine), vinegar/lemon juice, sour cream, chopped capers and a scattering of spices. You end up with a soup not short of either constituents or taste. There are all sorts of fanciful explanations of why the soup

is called "settlers". A common one is that "settlers soup" was often served up as part of the meal after the marriage ceremony and before the newly weds went off to "settle down" to their new life together!

2. **Herring under a Fur Coat** - basically this is a fish salad constructed in layers and called "selyodka pod shuboy" in Russian. The great World salads must include for example "Salad Nicoise' (France), "Waldorf Salad (USA), "Salad Olivier" (Russia), Caesar Salad (Mexico), "Tabboulah" (Lebanon) and "Greek Salad" (Greece) being just a few of the main examples. The skill of creating a decent salad, generally is not in cooking (for obvious reasons) but the making of perfect combinations such that the some of the parts is so much better than the constituents in isolation from each other. A successful salad is a ridiculously problematic creation unless you really understand how ingredients work together. A "Nicoise" is this fabulous combination of waxy potatoes, olives, tomatoes, green beans, egg plus anchovy or tuna (sometimes both). Never use fresh tuna it is the oily tinned stuff that works so well with the other salad ingredients. Salty anchovy and olives play their part by off setting the mild potato, egg and beans. In addition a "Caesar" is also a classic, balanced salad because it simply but effectively combines crunchy croutons with crispy lettuce mixed together in perfect harmony with an oily sauce and a scattering of Parmesan cheese. I consider that "herrings under a fur coat", though a much less well-known salad internationally, has

the hard to achieve blend of constituents that is the trademark of all the classics. Looking at the recipe, the key three items, loved by Russians are pickled herring, mayonnaise and fresh beetroot (part of the fur coat). All of which are good mates when together and strong tasting compared to the rest of the salad. The salad is layered in a ring with chopped boiled potato and some mayo first, then sliced onion, your chopped herring next with chopped boiled egg on top, then grated cooked carrot as a layer, plenty of mayo and boiled beetroot fine sliced as the top layer. Place the salad in the fridge to firm up and then it is ready to eat.

3. **Bird's Milk** - these days it is a delicacy that is admired throughout all of Russia; at least by those who are relatively well off and have heard of it. "Bird's milk" came into existence in Moscow at the one-time famous Praga restaurant. The Praga on Arbat Street has been around since the 19th Century and was the haunt of well-known writers and artists. It turns out the play write Anton Chekhov and the author Leo Tolstoy were regular visitors to Arbat Street. The Prada fell on hard times after the revolution when it was downgraded to a soup kitchen. However it was revitalized and during the latter part of the 20th Century became famous once again because of "bird's milk". The cake's Russian name is "ptichye moloko" and it was the brain-child of the pastry chef "Vladimir Guralnik" back in 1978. "Bird's milk" became so admired the recipe so it spread all over the country. It consists of a biscuit and mousse filling surrounded by a thin covering of chocolate.

Legend has it that "Guralnik" and his team could not get the mousse filling quite right and spent six months experimenting with different combinations and options. Hence it was considered in the end to be so exotic and ethereal it earned the right to be compared to milk from a bird (that is if birds ever were to produce milk). The home of "ptichye moloko" is no more sadly, the building that housed Praga was bought in 2018 by a Russian billionaire and mothballed.

4. **Easter** - now here we are talking about a rather exotic dish with an even more special name. The treat is called "Paskha" and that is the Russian word for Easter. The Orthodox Church requires its followers to fast for 40 days before Good Friday. On fast days there can be no meat or dairy and as these are fundamental to the Russian diet the "Great Lent" as it is called is no mean feat. It does mean that by the time Easter comes Russian Christians are lean and pretty hungry. Just as well because the Easter Festival is associated with some serious eating and celebrating. Russians do have eggs but not the chocolate type, they enjoy hens' eggs painted red. Some they exchange with friends, some they keep all year for luck and the rest they eat. Lamb, pork and turkey dishes are popular at this time as is sweet Easter bread. A most prominent dish is a cheese dessert, sometimes shaped as a truncated pyramid also sometimes it is topped by a lit candle. So revered is this dish that worshipers take it to church and is name is Russian for Easter itself "Paskha". It is a cheesy blancmange composed of a cheese curd called "tvorog"

that can be mimicked by using equal amounts of cream and cottage cheese. The dessert also contains butter, cream, eggs, currants, lemon peel, crushed nuts, candied fruits, sweets and spices. A massive dairy and sugar rush for the religious fasters who hadn't had dairy products for nearly 6 weeks?

POLAND

1. **Pie** - there is of course nothing odd or strange about a "pie", they have a prominent place in many cuisines. Surprisingly pastry-covered dishes may well have originated in England where they were originally called "coffins" with pastry that was inedible. The weird thing is that our Polish "pie" is a "bigos", an absolutely top-notch dish, but not in any way a "pie". "Bigos" is a stew and a remarkably variable one at that! It may well be on the menu of every Polish restaurant however "bigos" deep down in its very DNA is a classic of Polish home cooking. The meat component varies with what you have available, rabbit is common but pork and bacon are even more so. One type of meat, however, is a constant and that is the sausage - a nice meaty, garlic-rich Polish sausage. On the vegetable side, you need onion, more garlic, juicy tomato and even chopped fresh cabbage if you have some handy. Although the essential vegetable component is sauerkraut, pickled cabbage, and the water it is cooked in - a flavour creator for the stew. Our "bigos" originally was the product of whatever had been caught that day, hence the eclectic nature of the dish, an alternative name is "Polish hunter's stew". I once

worked at a Polish club in Central Scotland where I was provided with lunch. It was always "bigos" but from day to day never quite the same meal. "Pie" (or "hunter's stew") is a National dish of Poland but it is eaten all over the World these days.

2. **Little Pigeons** - I did not realise until I started putting this present collection of bizarrely named foods and meals together that there were so many World dishes named after birds that don't involve birds what so ever - and this is one of these. However if you are that way inclined, pigeons can be good eating. Although it has to be said they are not all that popular in modern Britain probably because of the masses of feral pigeons that mess our towns and cities. Of course no one eats these but actually there are two types of eating pigeon the wood pigeon and the squab. They are a common meal in several European countries where many enjoy the dark, tasty pigeon meat. The Poles have their pigeon dishes but "little pigeons", or more correctly "golabki", is definitely not one of them. "Golabki" are stuffed cabbage rolls making a typical weekly meal in Polish homes but they are just as common in countries near at hand such as the Ukraine, Russia, the Baltic States and Germany. The coverings for the "little pigeons" are boiled cabbage leaves irrespective of country. On the other hand, the filling does vary from place to place. Here in Poland "golabki" stuffing usually consists of a delicious combination of well-seasoned beef and pork mince mixed with onion and boiled white rice.

3. **Little Ears** - we have just been introduced to "little pigeons" (see previous) now we have "little ears" or in Polish "Uszka." These little tasty offerings are dumplings and Polish people do like their dumplings. After all, the whole Nation is fixated on "pierogi" irrespective what the filling happens to be. Sometimes these dumplings mostly have a savoury content such as seasoned mince, seafood mixtures, potato and cheese, sauerkraut and bacon although sweet fillings such as strawberries, fruit compote and lemon with sugar are not uncommon. Now, on the other hand, the midget eary "uszka", tend to have only one particular filling within their herby dumpling cover and that is a combination of chopped onion, breadcrumbs, egg white and finely diced mushroom. Mostly when you eat "pierogi" they are a dish in their own right along with a scattering of chopped green herbs and sour cream. On the other hand pan-fried "uszka" can be enjoyed on their own but tend to be better when accompanying other dishes, particularly soups. I've never been to Poland but I've eaten "uszka" alongside beetroot soup (the "borscht" that is so loved by Ukrainians, Russians and Poles). However it was in none of those places but in the old communist East Germany. It made a surprisingly rich and tasty meal that I thoroughly enjoyed. Polish friends and colleagues in the UK tell me that I would not get that combination of "borscht" and "uszka" in their home country except at Christmas. At other times of the year our dumpling "little ears" are usually served up alongside other soups usually the thinner options.

4. **Hooves** - no we haven't gone back to Portugal's "cow's hands" or even to horses hands or anything like that. "Hooves" are just another of the huge list of dumplings that are such an essential part of the Polish diet. Indeed they happen to be important to the cuisine of most, if not all, Eastern European countries. This stands in marked contrast to the standard meals of the bulk of Western Europe where the dough ball or dumpling is a curiosity rather than an essential constituent recognized by every one at suppertime as an old friend. An exception may well be Italy with their whole range of "gnocchi" and Holland with its traditional dishes such as chicken with dumplings. Although if you hop over the water to England its stew and dumplings was once a weekly essential that in recent decades has fallen out of favour through out the country. No such desertion happened in Poland however and our "hooves" turn out to be fairly small angular potato dumplings made from freshly cooked potato mashed in with egg, flour and salt. The Polish name for them is "kopytka" and usually they are served up with a topping of breadcrumbs fried off in butter. Personally I think the "hooves" look-a-like comparison in most instances stretches the imagination quite far but there again it is how you shape them when cutting your dumplings in the first place. Some Poles call "kopytka" "little fingers" and that may well be a better descriptive match. Outside Poland "kopytka" are frequently referred to as "Polish gnocchi" but as the Poles to my mind are the supreme dumpling makers perhaps instead "gnocchi" should be referred to as "Italian kopytka"?

SCANDINAVIA

1. **Flying Jacob** - I read an article in an American food magazine, apparently myopically focused on USA tastes, which included a list of what they considered horrific European dishes bound to offend the palate. The Swedish contribution to the US horror fest was "flying Jacob" or "flygande Jakob". Now that is a name that taxes the imagination so the Yank foodies have a point there. In addition the content is a bit on the unusual side I suppose. The dish is a kind of rough and ready rustic casserole that mixes chicken, chilli hot sauce, peanuts, bacon slivers and banana in a bed of cream that can then be cooked up in the oven. A scoop of "flying Jacob" is typically served up with a mound of rice and a side salad. Now given that one of America's top dishes is "chicken Maryland" consisting of fried chicken and banana plus the fact that banana wrapped in streaky bacon is a appetizer over there - I'm not at all sure what "flying Jacob" has done wrong! "It has been called a mish mash of this and that mostly by those who have never even tried it. Although unusual, the flavour combination is excellent - after all what's in it not to like! One downer I suppose is it is rather calorific so little

chance of taking flight after a big portion. The flying connection is down to the creator of the dish "Ove Jacobsson" who worked in aviation. "Flying Jacob" remains a café regular and a midweek treat in Swedish households stretching back to the 1970s when the recipe was first published.

2. **Cliff Fish** - sea fish, freshwater fish even flying fish but surely not cliff fish - what are they? These fish, it turns out, are a specialty from Norway ("klippfisk"). The Norwegians have been drying and salting cod going back to Viking times and salting fish and meat in general way back through history. An absolute essential if your country has short summers and very long and severe winters. There are numerous ways of preserving fish. Immersing them in vinegar is good such as is the fate of anchovies in the Mediterranean or herrings in the Baltic. You can salt cure your catch as is the case with "saltfish" or air-dry outdoors creating long lasting "stockfish" - stocks being the poles that carry the drying white fish (usually cod). Bacteria can't live in acid so that's how vinegar works, microorganisms don't cope with salt nor can they live without water so the fish lasts for quite some time. As a result it is worth considering salting your cod then letting it dry out also. It you do that you have fish that is as dry as a cliff and no longer likely to go bad. Now you have "klippfisk" in its very best storage form, not by any means its eating form. Basically your "klippfisk" has too much salt and hard as rocks - bad for bugs but bad for humans also. Before eating you need to get the salt

content way down and the meat much softer so your fish needs to soak for a day or so. There are loads of salt cod recipes in Norway and among the ones I know is a vegetable and "klippfisk" soup, a salt fish salad with boiled egg, tomato, onion and peppers, "cliff fish" including other salted cod preparations go well with potatoes or root vegetables and a "cliff fish" stew very like the Portuguese "bacalao stew".

3. **Slapped Ears** - we have had our "little ears" in the Polish section (see earlier) now they are about to get a good slapping. Finnish "slapped ears" or "korvapuusti" are sugar, cinnamon and cardamom buns that Fins love to eat with a nice cup of coffee or two. Of course the Fins are the World champion coffee drinkers par excellence. They go through a whopping 26 lbs /person/ year making the USA look coffee deprived (9 lbs/ person/year). As the Fins are the top coffee drinkers in the World, Finnish people must get through a massive number of "slapped ears". I think back to my boyhood and shudder! The mere mention of "slapped ears" compels me to form up in an imaginary queue with my ear cock up in the air. It all goes back to my School days in the South of Scotland; believe me that was not yesterday. As part of the educational process, the male teachers strapped our crossed hands with belts. The female teachers preferred slapping us repeatedly round the ears. Now the ear-slapping thing wasn't all that bad but the aftermath was. I have rather big ears that tended to light up after a decent slapping. "Here's Dumbo" was the predictable response from my so-called friends also

it is extremely hard to look cool with girls when your ears are glowing. "Korvapuusti" are so called because they are thought to look like "slapped ears". Well none of these people can have seen proper slapped ears and their buns are not bright red like my battered lugs. The Fins, think of their beloved buns as National treasures but it is a treasure shared with other Scandinavian countries who chew into "korvapuusti" at every opportunity. Perhaps that is because all of them are in the top six coffee drinking nations.

4. **Veiled Country Maiden** - several Scandinavian countries claim this dessert as being their own but I think Denmark has to be the main contender. To me at least, it is rather ironic given that Danish law has come down quite heavily on the use of veils. Not the wedding kind nor the country maiden version but the full veils worn by Islamic women. Denmark is not the only country in Europe to have such a ban (France and others) or partial ban (Norway for example) on wearing burqa-type veils in public. It seems to me more than a little ironic that face coverings for religious reasons are under attack while in these COVID times we are sensibly encouraging the use of medical styled masks for health reasons? The latter has to be right so where does that leave us with the former - or am I just being obtuse? Our dish is very tasty, if you like "apple Charlotte" then you will be right at home with "bondepige med slor". Get some cooking apples, water, plenty sugar, an abundance of breadcrumbs, crushed nuts, butter, red jam and whipped cream. Cook the apples with the water

and plenty sugar until you have a sweet puree. Melt the butter in a big frying pan and cook the breadcrumbs and crushed nuts until golden- stir in some sugar. Set the breadcrumb, nut and sugar mix also the apple puree to one side so they cool down. Take a dessert glass then layer in breadcrumbs followed by all the puree, more breadcrumbs, your jam, another breadcrumb layer and topped off with the whipped cream. Serve as cold as you can get it. Rather than the usual starter and mains, Danes like occasionally for their evening meal to substitute a thick hearty soup and a dessert instead. "Dondepige med slor" is a perfect dessert finisher to follow for example Danish chicken and meatball soup or their tasty split pea soup or even a filling potato soup perhaps? Whatever country soup our "veiled country maiden" will be happy with!

BALTIC STATES
AND BELARUS

1. **Hangover Soup** - I have never been there but I am told Belarus have very good beer and fierce vodka so it would appear to be a very good thing that they have a "hangover soup" for the next day. The soup is called "solyanka", the hangover thing is a nickname. It has a rather astringent sour taste so with a thumping head a bowl of this stuff will either put you back on your feet or finish you off completely either option being an improvement. Now "solyanka" translates as "salt soup" - so just as weird I guess. It is eaten in the Eastern regions of Germany where I have tried this soup a few times. I must admit not as a hangover cure though I often needed one. My suggesting this soup was born in Belarus will upset my Ukrainian friends enormously who think the sour soup is theirs. Having said that, others claim "solyanka" as being Russian. Lets just say if you have a banging head in Minsk the locals would direct you towards a bowl of "hangover soup" and leave it at that? Mind you if they were making the soup from scratch you will have a long wait! It is absolutely full of an enormous range

of ingredients. You want stock, probably beef, cubed fresh meat - beef and chicken will do, plenty of smoked sausage and a mixture of salted meats. Now add in plenty vegetables such as potato, onion, carrot, celery, cabbage and the like. In addition you need tomato as a paste, chopped black olives, capers, chopped dill pickle and plenty lemon. Throw in a glass of white wine dry as possible for good measure and you are done when it is cooked. Serve the soup with a dollop of sour cream. This soup in some cook's hands has such a sour edge it has the tartness of a stick of fresh rhubarb!

2. **Bread Soup** is a Latvian specialty that on the face of it seems pretty harmless though rather basic and subsistence living stuff. I suppose if you not much of an income and all you have in the larder a few slabs of old bread then turning it into soup is a sensible way to go. You will not starve; today at least! All nonsense of course because the dish is not a soup as we would know it but a very popular dessert in Latvia loved by everyone rich and poor alike. It is a family favourite comparable to the many bread puddings all over the World and especially the one so loved in Britain. Yes we Brits would be right at home with this dish in any of its forms. Basically it is stale rye bread grated to crumbs then soaked in hot water (you can try white wine) until it is soft and mushy. Now add sugar, lots of sugar, ground cinnamon as a dominant flavour and a little ground clove plus chopped up dried fruits (whatever you like). Cook in a pan on the hob till thoroughly warmed through then add some fruit juice - any will do. Serve up into dessert glasses and place in the fridge to cool. Before

serving, top with a little fiercely whipped cream and then you have a version of "maizes zoupa" or "bread soup". Yummy and definitely decadent don't you think?.

3. **Zeppelin** - in Lithuania, where this dish originates, it is known as a "cepelina" or as we would call it "a Zeppelin". After the Blitz in Britain and the total destruction of most German cities during WWII the civilian populations of Europe knew only too well the destructive power of aircraft raids. In WWI being bombed from the air was novel and came to England in the form of zeppelins. These huge balloons were terror weapons like the V rockets of WWII. The zeppelin raids were mostly ineffectual (not too the people killed and injured of course) but frightened the living daylights out of British civilians who became for the first time a strategic war target. The big oval shaped weapon was the talk of Europe to the extent that in the kitchens of Lithuania an ovoid potato dish was named "zeppelin". In all Baltic countries potatoes are a crucial part of the every day diet, but they are of particular importance in Lithuania. Our "cepelina" creation is made from raw grated potato with added onion dried out and pulped into a puree. The puree onion and grated potato mix is flattened and a substantial portion of raw mince or cream cheese is deposited on top. Thereafter it is rolled to form a potato coat and shaped to form a large "zeppelin-like" oval. The "zeppelins" are cooked in boiling water containing corn starch (keeps the "zeppelin" together during cooking). It is traditional to serve your "cepelina" with a sour cream sauce of your own choice.

4. **Rose Oil** - is the literal translation of an Estonian salad dish known as "rosoljie". I also believe an alternative, not so literal, Estonian meaning is colourful or cluttered. All Eastern European, Baltic and Scandinavian countries like a good potato salad and each place has its own variants. "Rosoljie" is one of several Estonian takes on the basic potato salad making it their own. I have enjoyed "rosoljie" on a number of occasions although not in its birthplace but in Finland and also along the Baltic coast of Sweden. Cooked and cubed salad potato is an obvious constituent but its distinctive "colour" and "rose oil" hue is down to the presence of beetroot. Some use picked others fresh but as there are other "sour constituents I prefer fresh. Perhaps because my mum loved fresh beetroot, sliced in a sandwich salted and doused in mayonnaise - she never made a mess! Other ingredients in "rose oil" salad include diced apple, chopped onion, finely sliced gherkin and of course chopped up best quality pickled herring. It is a Baltic dish after all! It is usually covered with a combination of mayo and sour cream (plain yoghurt will work instead of sour cream as an alternative). If you decorate the salad round the edges with slices of boiled egg, it produces an effective colour contrast to the dish. Eastern Europeans have a love for complicated potato salads ever since the birth of "Russian salad" in Moscow in the 19th Century. Over the decades their have been many variations arising in numerous countries so "rose oil" looks like one of these with "herring and beetroot" substituting for "chicken (or ham) and carrot" in the "Russian salad".

GERMANY

1. **Mouth Bags** - in Germany these, from times past, would be the feeding bags used to keep working horses nourished. I think in the UK the same leather construction filled with hay was called a nosebag. Dumplings and pasta in various forms play a central part of the German diet probably equally important to that of potatoes. One pasta dish, a specialty of the German region called "Swabia", is "maultaschen" which is a huge "ravioli-like" construction. They look like the product of a secret laboratory where the experiment went wrong and pretty little "ravioli" were turned into giant pasta monsters. Three things need to be said at this point; first Germans like their food to be on the substantial side, second "maultaschen" taste really good and third they do look like something horses might have over their mouths! "Maul" is the German word for an animal's mouth while a "tasche" is a bag. Take a sheet of pasta of a decent size and place your filling in the centre, fold over and form a pocket, egg wash and crimp the edges with your thumbs or a fork. Boil in a soupy broth or bake in a creamy mushroom sauce. The fillings can be various but usually involve spinach such as spinach,

potato and onion or spinach, breadcrumbs and cooked pork or even spinach with mince and herbs. If you visit Germany and want to try the dish, its home is in the southwest in an area known as Swabia whose biggest city is Stuttgart. and have the best food in Germany (no question). I think Swabian "mouth bags" are an unusual treat but in restaurants frequently they are called "Swabian pockets" because it drops the horse association and sounds a lot more appealing to tourists.

2. **Tree Frogs** - yes there is such a thing as tree frogs, not just one or two but there are hundreds of species all over the World. These little creatures usually have pads on their feet and one toe with a pointy nail that helps with their upwardly mobile climbing life style. Tree frogs are generally small with the largest being around five inches but some are less than an inch long. Now Germany has only one species of tree frog called the European tree frog which breeds in ponds but spends most of the year in the tree canopy or in bushes. On the other hand our edible "tree frogs" or "laubfrosche" is an affectionate name for the German style of cabbage rolls ("kohlrouladen"). A white cabbage is boiled up and the best and biggest leaves are used to wrap over a savoury beef mince, onion, breadcrumb and egg mixture somewhat like hamburger meat. The packages are tied with string and cooked in the oven then served up with gravy, a tomato sauce or on occasion a white sauce. Sometimes a serving is accompanied by rice but far better in my view are a few newly boiled potatoes. Very good eating on a cold day and a family treasure

for all year round. We have already met with a Polish roll called "little pigeons" (see earlier). Cabbage rolls, of variable content, pop up in many cuisines from those of Eastern Europe to the far reaches of South East Asia.

3. **Little Boy's Penis** - up to this point we have come across numerous parts of the anatomy including "headless larks" from France, "cow's hands" from Portugal including an assortment of ears from Poland and Finland (see earlier). However now we really are down to basics with little lads' private parts. I'm not at all sure what those ancient Popes, who spent an inordinately long time getting people to cover penises on statues with fig leaves, would have made of our dish? If you've been to the Vatican you will have seen all the fig leaves strategically placed. I read somewhere, that a student of Michelangelo, after the great man's death, got the job of making batches of modesty fig leaves. Clearly he didn't make enough because with some statues the offending member has been chiseled away - giving a new meaning to being struck off I suppose? Very nasty! However back to our German dish that turns out to be another set of little noodle-like dumplings called "bubenspitzle" at least that is their name in the southern state of Barvaria. These noodles are enjoyed all over Germany but elsewhere, more acceptably they are called "finger shaped noodles" "schupfnudeln". Our "little boys' penises" are rolled up little fingers of potato, flour, egg and a bit of spice are fried off in butter to make a delightful treat.

4. **Bee Stings** - wasps ok, I've been stung by them many times especially in late Summer and early Autumn when they get a bit drunk on over ripe fruit. I love fruit trees since I was a child when lived with my grandparents who had a small mixed orchard of around 100 trees. They had a single Victoria plum tree on its own that when in fruit was guarded by drunken wasps who thought it their property. I would rush in grab a plumb and rush out but it was not whether I got stung the only question was where! It's been like that ever since - wasps just don't like me and show it the way they know best! Bees on the other hand leave me alone, which is just as well because the very few times I have been stung by one I develop quite an amazing allergic reaction - like a red Mr Blobby. Wasps have a smooth stinger and can get you several times if you let it whereas the bee stinger is jagged and hard to remove. Lucky for me at least, our "bee sting" in question has nothing to do with aggravated insects; instead it is a rather enjoyable Barvarian dessert. More correctly it's a cake ("bienenstich kuchen") where the sweet brioche-type sponge has been split and the centre filled with heavily whipped and sugared cream. Alternatively the centre can be a rich confectioners custard or pastry cream. On top is a scattering of almond flakes and a rich honey or sugar syrup spread. Why name the cake "bee sting" for heavens sake? Well there are lots of fanciful tales but one I like says that once robbers attacked a village and throwing beehives at the thieves was an effective way to repel them! What to do with all that honey from broken hives. Well the local baker made cream buns liberally topped with honey. Delicious and problem solved!

AUSTRIA

1. **Cat's Tongues** - the thin, rather sweet biscuits are common in several countries particularly France. Certainly the flat crispy biscuits look rather tongue-like when they come out of the oven and are best eaten fresh. It maybe the little flat biscuits are French, Dutch or even Spanish in origin. Sorry France and the rest, I have given the sweet biscuit to the Austrians. Austria over the centuries has been the baking innovator of Europe. Whereas other Western European countries have been sufficiently sneaky to claim Austrian creations as their own - that may also be the case for cats tongue biscuits. The French like to tell everyone the croissant and the baguette is theirs but in fact Austrian bakers introduced both to that country. We enjoy Danish pastries but they also are Austrian rather than Scandinavian - get the drift? I remember the crisp "cat's tongue" biscuits from visits to Vienna were they are known as "katzenzungen"; a name common to all German speaking peoples. "Katzenzungen" part covered with chocolate are ace! In France they are called "langues de chat" whereas in Holland they are "katte tong". A great Dutch café treat is fresh "katte tong", a scoop of ice cream and a cup of decent coffee. The Dutch in colonial times

made the sweet treats in far away South East Asia whereas the Spanish took them to South America.

2. **Emperor's Pancake** - it isn't some brainless royal doing a belly flop into a swimming pool although it sounds something like that. No the pancake is a pudding, not the thin versions seen in the UK mostly on "Shrove Tuesday" but a substantial Germanic affair that fills a huge frying pan and is chopped up into bits. One time my companion and I were at "St. Christoph" in the Austrian Alps staying at a mountain top hotel. One evening, to my companion's dismay, the special dinner turned out to be wild boar and dumplings (neither to her taste). A friendly waitress delivered to her a vast frying pan, detached the handle and there was nicely chopped up "emperor's pancake" or "kaiser (emperor) schmarrn (shredded)". The dish it seems has several different names but I guess "emperor's pancake" is preferable to "shredded emperor" at least. Going back to the meal St Christoph, I have to say several of us abandoned the meat and dumplings to help out with the vast but tasty pancake treat coated liberally with icing sugar. The owner of our hotel told us that the dish had originally been created for the Empress but she found it too rich. On the other hand the husband, Emperor Franz Joseph I, thought the pancake delightful so rather than her it was named after him instead. As well as big lumps of light pancake dusted in sugar there is a scattering of alcohol-soaked raisins and a pouring of fruit compote. In this case a tart plumb sauce that brought balance to the dish. A few days later we stopped off in Munich for

a city break. Deep into January this is often a cold place to be except if you are by a roaring fire eating "emperor's pancake". We had learned that this Austrian pudding was dearly loved in Bavaria also. Certainly it was not hard to find on displayed eating-place menus and came with apple as well as plum compote. Much as we loved this treat we decided that summer holidays were far more preferable to winter breaks!

3. **Cheesy Little Sparrows** - no it isn't "cheeky little sparrows" the spelling is correct it is "cheesy little sparrows" or "kasespaetzle". The dish has been called the Austrian version of "mac and cheese" and I have to say it is just as tasty. Now the basic pasta in the dish, the "spaetzle" are part of the cuisine of all the German speaking counties and probably were first made in "Swabia" an area famous for its rustic but inventive cooking (see "mouth bags" previously). However when you add in cheese and onions to the pasta, then you have a delicacy specific to Austria. The dish is a restaurant regular but can also be made at home in your kitchen from scratch. Mix flour eggs, a little water and salt to make a viscous but somewhat loose dough that needs to rest a while. Cook on low heat some onions in butter and when soft set aside. Now heat up a pan of water to simmer and then take your dough. Experts make "spaetzle" by snipping off little bits of dough and dropping it into the water. Don't despair there is an easy way to make "little sparrows" drop your soft dough into a colander and little sparrows of dough will drop through the holes and cook in the water. They only

need 2 or 3 minutes then remove the hot "spaetzle" with a slotted spoon and mix with an abundance of grated cheese and the soft onions. Add some green herbs (parsley is good), plenty seasoning and the dish is ready.

4. **Mozart Balls** - is a totally ridiculous name but I always seem to buy them in Austrian airport shops to take home. "I've just been to Vienna, here is a box of "Mozart balls", you hand them over without a second thought as they are Austrian to the core even having the picture of the great composer on the wrapper covering each sweet. Now I've past by thousands of boxes of these little fellows and bought quite a few I have to say. It is not until recently I have thought about how incongruous and dare I say inappropriate is the name of this over abundant confection. There cannot be a tourist shop or tourist location in Vienna that doesn't have loads of boxes of "Mozart balls" or "Mozartkugel" on display ready for the heavy sell. Although the shopkeepers don't need the heavy sell to hook me in - I'm a dark chocolate over marzipan freak. Nougat and nuts add to the temptation. If I ever had a spooky hypothetical conversation with Mozart he would surely want to talk about music whereas all I would want to do is complement him on his chocolates. Unfortunately he didn't invent the confection, though it came into being in the composer's hometown of Salzburg in the 1890s. Paul Furst was the creator of these tasty morsels in honour of the town's best-known son. After all, Beethoven, Chopin. Wagner, Bach and the rest of the gang of genius composers failed in the business of having a decent marzipan chocolate named after them.

CZECH (NOW CZECHIA) AND SLOVAK REPUBLICS

1. **Grenadier March** - this is a Slovakian dish called in that country "granadirsky pochod". Slovakia has only become a country in its own rite in recent years (1993) before that it was part of Czechoslovakia and back before that it was the northern part of Hungary and a component of the Austro-Hungarian Empire. Slovakia supplied more than its share of soldiers to support the aspirations of an aggressive empire. The Slovakians also provided numerous recruits who would become grenadiers. In more modern times there are grenadier regiments but initially some grenadiers were attached to general infantry regiments. Grenadiers were always the biggest and strongest of any soldiers around them. They had to be because their job was to get up close and personal to enemy barricades and knock them down or blow them up. These men had a high opinion of themselves probably quite rightly. They would expect the best of food "an army marches on its stomach", so it holds that "granadirsky pochod" must be a really rich and meaty delight then? As it turns out this 19th Century creation is a cheap and rather economical

vegetarian dish that would be despised by our grenadiers when they were served it up in their military canteens. "Grenadier march" is essentially a carbohydrate-rich belly filler that is a mash up of precooked potatoes with pasta squares made tasty by an abundance of fried onions, paprika and a pickled gherkin or two. "Granadirsky pochod" survived over the years, in recent times not as a special in veggie restaurants but as a standard school dinner, a works canteen filling meal and an end of week economy dinner at home. There are numerous basic dishes that have tongue in cheek names such as "Welsh rabbit" that is just cheese on toast while "soldiers" are just slices of toast you dip in egg. More than likely "grenadier march" is a laugh at those who would not touch this vegetarian dish with a barge pole. That the dish "granadirsky pochod" is a not too popular school dinner does not bode well. However a plate of "granadirsky pochod" tasted quite nice to me especially with spicy sausage on the side. It is a very carb-rich meal but still it is full of flavour. Like many plain foods, it can be prepared well or very badly I guess. I do think these Slovakian soldiers and school kids were wimps. After all they did not have to cope with "turkey twizzlers" or "tapioca pudding" fed to my children when they were at school.

2. **Small Pockets** - possibly better than deep pockets and short arms! This dish has German overtones but also it is a Czech favourite you see listed on most restaurant bar menus and also it is a standout café regular. "Kureci kapsa" is fried or grilled chicken breast stuffed with masses of ham and cheese. There is a definite "pocket"

cut into the chicken flesh by the chef but I'm not at all sure if the "small" part of the name is at all accurate especially after the rather large opening is stuffed to overflowing with salty ham and processed cheese slices. Ok we are not dealing with anything top drawer here nor even are "small pockets" a longstanding traditional Czech specialty. It is what it is, a quick evening dinner where bland chicken is made immeasurably tastier and moister by the meat and cheese stuffing. Served up with mash, potato salad or chips and in some recipes smothered with a creamy mushroom sauce (you must have the sauce if they have it, if not get a side dish of mushrooms to complement the main dish). Dry or sauced, "small pockets" is a meal a hundred times better than a franchise "hamburger and fries" or the ubiquitous "hotdog". Would I eat this dish? Well it's a modern Czech classic but also basically a tourist special so what is there to dislike? I've filled up on "small pockets" many times in Prague; a city where the architecture is glorious, the people are welcoming and more importantly the beer is cheap. You need something substantial but not too exotic to soak up the booze when you are bar hoping in the Czech Republic. Tip from me- bar hop all year round except Winter, especially January, often minus something silly that month. I did a January bar hop in Prague and lost the feeing in my toes for days after.

3. **Moravian Sparrow** - currently this dish is a multinational classic, enjoyed by many throughout Eastern Europe. The territory that was Moravia is now the southern part of the Czech Republic but in times past Moravia was

wedged between Bohemia (Czech lands) and Slovakia and all three had lots in common including shared cuisine. Czechs would be horrified at the suggestion that "Moravian sparrow" is Slovakian in origin. The best recipes for "Moravian sparrow" are from Slovakia as far as I can glean and it was the place I first had the dish so there! "Moravsky vrabec" is not complicated in any way but when cooked with a bit of love and care, it is superb. I've travelled a great deal in Eastern Europe but my time in Slovakia has been short so far. In my whole lifetime I managed to spend only a single day and night in that country. I gave a research presentation at a medical meeting held in a hotel in North West Slovakia. I'm not at all sure what I talked about as this was one of a number of stopovers in Europe on an international tour of lectures. However I absolutely do remember my hosts treated me that evening to "moravsky vrabec" as part of their conference dinner. I once knew a teacher called Doctor Vrabec and now I know he was a Doctor Sparrow! The dish is good quality chopped pork in spicy cumin and paprika gravy accompanied by slices of bread dumpling and sauerkraut. Perfect eating! I know it is not for everyone but I am a sauerkraut lover. Sauerkraut is of course found everywhere in Eastern Europe and also Northern Continental Europe but did not come from there. Way back in time sauerkraut was a nutritious meal for the workers who built the Great Wall of China (they started work over 200 years B.C.). The vinegary cabbage dish suited the tastes of the Mongol hordes who brought death and destruction to Europe in the 13th Century and left behind sauerkraut when their marauding was over.

4. **Drowning Men** - got to be a novelty for men from the Czech Republic after all it is a land locked country! However the place is riddled with small lakes and transected by many magnificent rivers. The mighty Elbe (flows hundreds of miles north through Germany to the North Sea) and the Oder (flows through West Poland to the Baltic) both originate in the Czech Republic. These "drowning men" you will not find in the rivers and lakes of the country side but ensconced in the abundant cities and towns. Indeed they exist in almost every inn and tavern in the Czech Republic. I made a big deal about "small pockets" being pub grub but "drowning men" without doubt is the ultimate in Czech bar food in this part of the world. You ask for "utopeneci" and you get "bratwurst" but really heady "bratwurst sausage" that have been cooked in a strange way. The sausages are boiled in a vinegar-rich marinade - so while they are cooking they look like they are "drowning men". The delicacy has been around for 100 years or so. It is well-established pub grub that is popular with the locals brought up on these tit bits and a real pickled sausage challenge for the braver more adventurous tourists (who needs a pickled egg or a gherkin if you have one of these!). They are served up with thick slabs of bread and a dollop of strong mustard. There is however a dark side to the tale with several sources suggesting that the inventor himself took his own life by drowning. Truth or fiction the black story has helped make a weird sausage cooking technique keep its equally odd name of "drowning men" over the decades.

HUNGARY

1. **Snail** - yes snails have been part of the Hungarian diet since Roman times but the real ones are by no means as popular as the bakery version we are considering here. Not so much a garden snail as a baked chocolate snail or in Hungarian "kakaos csiga" because of the rolled up appearance of the pastry. I guess you get them throughout the whole country but certainly in the capital Budapest they are a common snack to have with your morning coffee. The lengths of sweet dough are bound tightly together in a spiral by rich, dark cocoa butter glue. If you think of the love child that might come if a regular Danish became intimate with a French chocolate croissant - then you have a reasonable idea of the composition and texture of this Hungarian treat. Mind you, I have to wonder (it's the way my mind works) if Danish pastries had been called Danish snails whether we would be eating them with such relish in every part of the World. While we are on such trivial pursuits did you know that Danish pastries are called Danish everywhere in the World except Denmark? In that country they are Vienna pastries because they are actually Austrian in origin. Mind you I did go on

pursuit of Vienna pastries on a raining day in that town only to find there was no such thing but I could get a Danish almost everywhere?

2. **National Assembly Soup** - I find Hungary to be a place of thick soups and thin stews so if you lump them all together then you have an extraordinary number of dishes best eaten only when you have a decent sized spoon handy. The thick meaty stew called "goulash' for instance in its place of origin, Hungary, is served up as a soup eaten in a bowl. National Assembly soup ("orszaggyules leves") also is a fairly robust creation in that very Hungarian mold of soupy stews or stewy soups. The Hungarian National Assembly Building, or Parliament Building, is in the capital Budapest located on the Pest side of the River Danube and is where the National Assembly people meet. I had been told it was built on a design based on the British Houses of Parliament. You can see some likenesses but the Hungarian version looks as if it had taken to the dungeons and stretched for a while on a ginormous rack. It is an enormously tall building. You would need a bowl or two of "National Assembly soup" to get up to the top I suspect. Now if you assumed, as I did, that it was a special soup created for Members of the Assembly (MPs) then that is wrong. The soup is complex and quite diverse in content rather like the make up of the Hungarian Assembly I suppose. Hence the name? It contains smoked and processed meat (smoked sausage like "kolbasz" plus spiced and processed meats), vegetables (particularly carrot) and diverse dried fruits

(apple, pear, plumb, peach and others) so it is rich and a meal in its own right, starter, main course and pudding all within one rather large bowl!

3. **Seven Chiefs** - way back in time, the 9th Century, perhaps earlier, the Magyars, a nomadic group of peoples from Northern Europe travelled south to settle around the upper to middle Danube area. These travellers covered a lot of ground to get to their eventual home coming from what today are north Russian into southern Finnish territories. As such the nearest language to Hungarian anywhere in the World is Finnish. There were seven tribes that made up the original confederation and their leaders are commemorated in many ways but one of those is through our dish. "Seven chiefs" is a "tokany" one of a number of Hungarian names for a stew. Among the pantheon of thick soups and stews that Hungary has in abundance, "het vezer tokany" is at least to me, the one I like far more than most including the internationally famous "goulash". There are superb home-cooked brilliant versions of "het vezer tokany" but it also lends itself to being a restaurant masterpiece (I know that sounds hopelessly condescending but really it is not meant that way). I had the dish at Grundel's Restaurant outside the City Park in Budapest and it was the best I ever tasted but my companion said her Mum made a far better version - you get the drift? The Grundel recipe contains beef, pork, veal and smoked bacon, tomato, onion, peppers plus loads of paprika and sour cream. A green salad, herbs and soft dumplings help complete

the dish. Absolutely and ridiculously decedent as are most of the other recipes I have seen for this dish. It needed to feed seven chieftains s after all and it is said that each one contributed to the final meal!

4. **Chimney Cake** - given that there are so many unusual dishes with fanciful names in Hungarian cuisine, this one maybe not quite in the top drawer of odd names. Granted it is a weird name for a cake but as it looks like a chimney it is exactly what it claims to be. My first taste of "chimney cake" was just after communism had been ousted probably in the early 1990s or there about. I was in the southern city of Sopron while a festival was on and some stall-holders were selling freshly made "chimney cake" or "kurtoskalacs". Sweet dough was rolled out thin and wrapped around a greased pole or some such structure and then cooked. The bread/cake is further sweetened - mine had cinnamon and sugar (delicious). I thought they were local or Austrian given the closeness to the border. I was to learn from a friend that I was entirely wrong. The dish it seems to have originated in the Hungarian speaking part of Transylvania from way back. No one really knows how many centuries the cake has been around but a lot. "Kurtoskalacs" is claimed both by Hungary and Rumania and these days, in a myriad of different forms, it is enjoyed as street food, a simple café treat or a home-cooked delight. In the modern world, chimneys are on the way out hardly useful anymore but in Britain at least they are still part of the skyline as a reminder of times past. A friend from Miami came

to London so I showed him the many attractions of that big City. "What impressed you most?" I asked at the end of the first sightseeing day. Immediately he responded "chimneys and so many of them! I've never seen chimneys before!".

BALKANS

1. **Black George** - way back in the 18th Century there was a Serbian leader who went by the name of "Karadjordji" that translates to "Black George". During his time Serbia and the surrounding countries were under the thrall of the Ottoman Empire who were by no means enlightened occupants of the country. Our "Black George" was essentially a Serbian revolutionary who fought the Turks with considerable venom, freeing much of the country and becoming its supreme leader and given the title of prince. However "Karadjordji" was assassinated so the freedom was only temporary. After his death he was eulogized and heralded as the "unifier of all Serbian peoples". I don't know how the dish "Black George" came to be called after the revolutionary but there are lots of inns and restaurants named after the hero so perhaps that is the connection? Essentially "Black George" is a substantial veal cutlet or pork fillet rolled out thin and flat and smeared with local cream cheese, on top goes a layer of ham and then more cheese. Carefully roll up the meaty, cheesy bundle and pin with toothpicks or string. Coat thickly with flour, egg and breadcrumbs and deep fry. Slice

up and serve with sour cream, tartar sauce and salad. A substantial enough dish for a hungry revolutionary prince or even a starving traveller.

2. **Snow White** - we all know the story. According to the Grimm brothers fairy tale the queen of a far off land had a daughter with hair black as ebony, lips as red as blood and skin as white as virgin snow. Sadly the queen died after childbirth and the king, as kings are prone to do, married a beautiful but truly frightful new queen proud and totally cruel - nasty times for Snow White as it turned out. The step mum hated "Snow White", she was too pretty to survive. However survive she did with the help of seven dwarfs and the nasty queen got her comeuppance. Passing from Germany fairy tales to Bulgarian cuisine our princess turns into a salad called "snezhanka" or "Snow White". The combination of cucumber and fresh yoghurt is classic and essentially the basis of our Bulgarian dish. Slice cucumbers in half and remove watery seeds, chop into chunks. You can add some fine chopped pickle also. Take strained, and therefore very thick, plain yoghurt and mix in some olive oil and lemon juice plus chopped dill and three cloves of grated garlic. Spread all over the cucumber and fold in. Scatter crushed walnuts on top and you have refreshing "Snow White" salad. You might think you have seen this dish before and you would be right as it is a part of every cuisine between Greece and India and more besides but they don't call it "Snow White"!

3. **Small Ones** - I'm not as familiar with Romanian dishes as I should be given I once tried to buy a small farmhouse there complete with vines (Romania is a big wine producer). It was not one of my more sensible ventures, if I ever have such things, so we will leave it at that. I have a number of Romanian friends and also past work colleagues who have an enthusiasm for home cooking and have teased me about this slight gap (alright gaping hole) in my knowledge. I appreciate from them and others that Romanian cuisine is sophisticated with influences ranging from Turkey to Germany. However if asked what is my most loved Romanian dish I always reply "mici" because that is all I know! Now this dish is not fine dining by any stretch of imagination but it is a Rumanian food cliché in the same way England is to "pork pies", USA and their "hotdogs" or being an Australian with a "vegemite sandwhich". "Mici" when spoken aloud sounds like (m-ee-ch) and there is an alternative name "mititei" and both names translate to "small ones". Now "mici" are not that minute being several inches long and basically kofte-related. "Mici" have a sausage shape but lack a skin covering so that limits their size. Indeed it was suggested that they were invented in a restaurant that had run out of sausage skins. To me they have burger or meatball consistency. Really a burger with attitude containing lots of seasonings, garlic, some thyme and local herbs in a mix of beef, lamb and pork mince. As street food, they are served up with bread and mustard while in a café setting there are always accompanied by lots of chips and a little salad.

4. **Under the Bell** - around the World there are some serious bells such as the Tsar Bell in Moscow from the 18th Century and weighing a ridiculous 180 tons! In Japan there is the Great Bell of Kyoto coming in at a whopping 116 tons. They both make Great Paul, our biggest bell housed in St Paul's Cathedral, a mere anorexic at a puny 16 tons. You can get into the Tsar Bell (it has a door) and get under the other two bells but you definitely can't cook using any of these big characters. Our "under the bell" is not so much a specific dish but a Croatian way of cooking meat and vegetable stews. In Croatian the cooking procedure is called "ispod cripnje" ("under the bell") while an alternative name is "peka", which I am told simply means to bake. Now as an alternative to oven cooking and back in times when ovens were not available but oven style cooking was possible with a decent pot that has a heavy lid sitting on a wide fire hearth. Some say "under the bell" is the whole pot but I have a sneaky feeling it refers to the heavy lid that may have been dome or bell shaped and of course lies on top of the food. A typical content of the pot would be lamb shanks, goat or even seafood like octopus supplemented by root vegetables, potatoes, loads of onions, herbs and a few spices plus a good glug of wine or stock. This type of dish is served all over Croatia. "Under the bell" cooking holds its own, in a nice smoky way, with a Western European heavy pot casserole or a US Dutch oven dish. By the way Dutch ovens were first created in Bristol not Holland - I wonder if they were based on cooking "under the bell"?

GREECE AND IT'S ISLANDS

1. **Bubbler** - the blubberers are not a treat for the vast majority of Brits but loved smothered with hot garlic butter in France while in Spain they are one of the original constituents of "paella". Our dish here, called "bubbler" or "bourbouristi" on Crete, is fried snails and the locals consider them a special delicacy. Although not highly regarded by the majority of visitors and tourists who are often from the UK. I'm not all that sure why we have an aversion to these things but in Britain we haven't really eaten them since Roman times when they were not a delicacy but a staple. I've been to Alicante many times because I had a holiday home nearby. One Sunday I was walking down a side street when I bumped into some locals I knew. They were cooking a ginormous paella on an outside fire. I donated a couple of bottles of wine and joined them for lunch. They concocted a traditional style Valencia paella dish with rabbit, chicken and snails in a slow cooked pan of rice and vegetables. One of the best afternoons I have ever had until I found out that grandpa had not bought

our snails from a shop (clean) but had plucked them from the garden wall that morning (dodgy disease wise). On Crete the largest of the Greek Islands, their special "kohli bourbouristi" is a frying pan of snails in their shells drenched in salt, olive oil and herbs. The name comes from the sounds the frying snails make in the cooking pan where they are said to make a bubbling, popping noise. A far cry from our well-known "bubble and squeak" (see England earlier) but much the same idea I guess.

2. **Pharmacist** - I'm cheating a little here because the odd name is "spetzieriko" known to be derived from the word "spetsieri" a pharmacist. "Spetzieriko" is not the dish itself but the spice mix used to flavour the dish rather in the same way in other parts of the World cooks use "garam masala" (India), "ras el hanut" (North Africa), "five spice" (China) and "curry powder" (UK). For our "spetzieriko" we look to the Greek Island of Corfu that is actually a product bought by locals at pharmacies on the Island if not made up at home. Corfu today is known as a beautiful holiday destination whereas in its past it has been a stronghold and a holding centre for Venetian spice trade. Venice held Corfu for 400 years so Italian influences are strong both in Island culture and diet. Corfu folks like their pasta so one of their top dishes with Italian overtones is the Sunday special known as "pastitsada". It is a beef, tomato and red wine stew sweetened with lots of onion and garlic. It is heavily flavoured with plenty "spetzieriko". The spice mixture is infinitely variable and complex. Although you would

expect it to have cinnamon, cloves, paprika, nutmeg, sometimes cumin, bay and black pepper. It is said the ingredients can get up to fifteen or more in some recipes so no wonder there is a role for a pharmacist. The slow cooked "spetzieriko"-flavoured beef stew is accompanied by long pasta. "Spaghetti" is all right but the tubular "bucatini" holds the meaty sauce better. A scraping of hard cheese on top completes the dish. There is a second recipe for "pastitsada" that uses cock hens and onions stewed in wine and it is suggested that this is considered locally as the economy version. Historically those who selected the cock hen "pastitsada" were people who found spice mixtures unaffordable. As an alternative, lots of locally plucked herbs became the cheap option so creating a quite different tasting "pastitsada" dish. These days this Corfu classic has a wider fan base. I have seen both dishes on line and in recipe books. The beef option with its rich spice mix is evident but rather strangely the cock hen alternative is often given a good spice exposure. Personally I think the cock hen dish is better with herbs but if you go for spices then dampen it down somewhat because the full "spetzieriko" is far too powerful for fowl even a tasty cock hen. Beware the "pharmacist" is quite overwhelming with anything but the most robust meats.

3. **Shoes** - there are big overlaps between the cuisines of different countries especially adjoining counties with close social and historical links. Northern Ireland, Scotland, Wales and England have most of their dishes in common, the Scandinavian countries also have

more in common than different with respect to their dishes. German and Austrian cuisines are cousins while Russia and Ukraine argue about who came up first with their multitude of common food items. However Greece belonged to the Ottoman Empire their cultures, if not their religions, became inextricably linked. On independence the Greeks made huge efforts to be separate in everything including having their own cuisine. So for example hummus and moussaka became part of Greek national identity. Hummus is not Greek but originated in the Arab World while the inspiration for moussaka is Turkish. A Greek chef merely topped the Ottoman dish with béchamel. Thus so it is that "shoes" is essentially the dish you will see in the Turkish cook books as the "Imam has fainted" (see later) with a topping of béchamel. Worked once lets do it again but this time lets call it something entirely different. So when in Greece you half your aubergine fill the centre with mince and chopped tomato then top it off with that classic French sauce, béchamel so loved by Greeks. The dish then becomes "papoutsakia" rather than "Imam bayaldi". On behalf of the Greeks I think the dish does look like a shoe so they are spot on there but I would suspect any priest would faint after having to eat a "shoe".

4. **Bread of Basil** - you are forgiven for thinking that this is probably not one of this book's strangest names. Except the present delicacy doesn't contain the herb basil and although Greeks in the past enjoyed it as a loaf, these days it is, more often than not, a delicious cake called

"vasilopita". Not for the first time in this collection we have a dish that is associated with an important celebration but this time it is New Year. The Basil, it turns out, is a really important Greek Orthodox Saint - St Basil. The saint's feast day is 1st January so I suppose that's why the cake is named after him. You may not of heard of Basil of Caesarea, a religious leader from way back (4th Century A.D.), but he was one of the leading lights in the formation of the Greek Orthodox Church. He was a rock who held back Western Christianity ideas from taking off in the Eastern Orthodox world. Maybe Basil was not the most loved priest but he was among the most admired and respected. My "bread of Basil" therefore turns out to be a more than decent orange-flavoured sponge cake with a glaze topping. The treat is for communal family eating so buried within the cake should always be a high denomination coin. If you get the slice with the money therein then you are expected to have good luck for the whole year (and perhaps a hefty dental bill?). Its rather ironic that Saint Basil, a bit of a tough nut in his day, is best known in Greece for a gooey New Years cake. The double irony is that he was Turkish and given the historical enmity between these two countries it is strange that he is better known in Greece than Turkey.

OTHER MEDITERRANEAN ISLANDS

1. **Widow's Soup** - at various times the Island of Malta has been a fortress in the Mediterranean and during WWII it became Britain's unsinkable aircraft carrier. Unsinkable it may be but the Axis air forces tried their best to flatten it over the war years. The capital and main port, Valetta, is a beautiful place but after walking about the streets you still see some of the remaining scars of the continuous bombing and strafing. The city is compact and it is hard to imagine that more bombs hit Valletta than the whole of London during the Blitz! The Island's hardship was not confined to non-relenting air attacks because both disease and starvation were also close companions to the people and military alike. The Island was blockaded, so little in the way of food or medicines got through. The locals needed to farm what they could, forage where possible, fish sporadically at high risk and grow vegetables and fruit anywhere the soil was fertile. Several economy meals from the traditional Maltese cuisine came to the fore during these harsh times, one being "widow's soup". An ideal

inexpensive dish to use up a range of economic easy grown vegetables and be both healthy and nutritious at the same time. The "soppa tal-armla" (or "widow's soup") was made often during the War especially by the older women too many of whom had lost their partners. It has to be said however the name goes back far into Malta's past. It is a vegetable soup based on the combination of onions, garlic, kohlrabi, cauliflower, carrots, potatoes, beans and the like. Tasty then but in present day Malta it is usual to embellish the one time peasant soup with local cheese and or eggs to make it special! Britain, also under siege during WWII, still loves some of the war economy specialties like "toad in the hole" and "apple crumble" that today are also more luxurious dishes than once was the case.

2. **Dirty Rice** - I guess many of you will be saying what is so special about "dirty rice"? After all it is a common US dish present on many American restaurant menus that originated as a Cajun delicacy from Louisiana. The classic dish is cooked in chicken stock along with Cajun spice, chopped vegetables, pork mince and fine chopped chicken livers and other chicken bits such as gizzard. The fine chopped meat, the veg and the spice make the white rice look less than pristine so giving the rice its "dirty" name. "Dirty rice" has become a common dish throughout America and for that matter it has appeared wherever in the World American dishes are enjoyed. These days the key chicken liver and gizzard constituents are often replaced by less demanding meat options. There is however on the Mediterranean island

of Mallorca a "dirty rice" that has nothing to do with Cajun cuisine and the US state of Louisiana. Mallorca is the largest of the Spanish Balearic Islands with a population close on one million people greatly boosted during the popular tourist months. The Island has a cuisine that is partly traditional Spanish but also it has it's own distinctive dishes an example being their very own version of "dirty rice". The rice dish called "arroz brut", as is the case with Cajun "dirty rice", is basically a member of the "pilau" family. "Pilau" is essentially a spicy, fluffy stock-cooked rice often enriched with vegetables and some meat. Our Majorcan "arroz brut" is a highly regarded local creation with no International reputation other than being enjoyed by locals and the mass of tourists that visit the island. It consists of rice cooked with cinnamon, paprika, cloves, saffron and nutmeg. The meat these days is usually chicken or pork but traditionally it was rabbit or even snails. The vegetables are just as variable also being anything immediately at hand from mushrooms to beans and usually there are plenty of peppers. The key distinguishing feature of "arroz brut" from "Cajun dirty rice" and other "pilaus" is that there is extra stock in the cooking liquor so the finished dish is sloppy in a nice but unusual way - a soupy consistency. It has been a recognized dish in Mallorca from the 14th Century when the Moors brought it probably as a rice-thickened stew for using up game and offal. These days the content of "arroz brut", other than rice and spice, change with the seasons but still is better eaten with a spoon than a fork!

3. **Breadcrumbs** - we all know what "breadcrumbs" are and that they are one way of using up stale loaves. In fact "breadcrumbs" have multiple uses ranging from being a good thickener for stews to serving as a coating to protect fried fish and meat. In Sardinia "breadcrumbs" are "breadcrumbs" but also they are something else as I found out to my surprise and amusement on my first visit to that Italian Island. I had been working in the inland city of Sassari for a couple of days and then set off for the coast. A priority was to get a nice meal having lived on college food since my arrival. My few words of café menu Italian had not increased since arriving here but I did know "frutti di mare" was seafood and "fregola" were breadcrumbs. So a dish of seafood in breadcrumbs, presumably deep fried, was very much to my taste. In the end I was served prawns, shellfish and squid rings mixed into what looked like over sized "cous cous". Sardinians, it turned out, do like their pasta and an Island favourite they call "fregola" because it is "breadcrumb" size. In the world of Italian pasta the different types typically are named after their appearance. For example "campanelle" do look like little bells (sort of), "conchiglie" are shell-shaped (definitely), "farfalle" have a butterfly appearance (to me they are bows) and "rotelle" are wheels (even down to the spokes). Apart from size however it is hard to imagine spherical "fregola" as being anything like "breadcrumbs" in appearance. They are a pasta of tiny balls made from "semolina" dough rather like North African "berkoukes" that goes into spicy soups.

"Fregola" is equally good in soups, pasta salads and numerous Sardinian main meal dishes.

4. **Sorrows** - are cheese buns from Cyprus one of the largest of the Mediterranean islands. Cyprus is divided into a Turkish North eastern portion and a Greek South Western segment. Essentially this special treat comes from the Greek side of the Island and is best known by its Greek name "flaounes" that roughly translates as "sorrows". Most of these buns or pies are eaten at Easter to the extent that they are completely associated with that celebration. "Flaounes" go back to the 19th Century when, and thereafter, were baked in abundance on Holy Saturday. Saturday was the day when Christians believe the body of Jesus was laid in his tomb. The number of treats prepared by each family was always excessive so the leftovers were taken to Church on Sunday morning to be given to the poor and elderly or anyone who were unable to bake their own "sorrows". The mass bake off of the buns/pies is specific to Holy Saturday. Sometimes that day is called Black Saturday being a traditional day of mourning, and that might explain the "sorrow" name. The bread buns can be savoury (chopped olives and herbs) or sweet (currants, sultanas and spices) but always contain cheese (haloumi and other harder varieties).

TURKEY

1. **The Imam has Fainted** - a so much better name than the Greek copy of the same dish that the Greeks called "shoe" (see earlier). It is still essentially sliced and hollowed aubergine, stuffed with an onion, tomato, garlic plus other goodies and then baked. This is, certainly to me, a clear case of less in much more. Between you and I the toping of béchamel sauce that characterizes the Greek variety just doesn't work so I go for "Imam bayaldi" every time. The story goes that the dish is so delicious even an Imam (a holy man) would pass out with delight when eating it! I used to show off in years past by serving up the dish at dinner parties and I remember that many guests did pass out but, more likely, that was the result of excess gin and whisky rather than tasty aubergines. The Turkish creation ("Imam bayaldi") is now Worldwide but enjoyed particularly throughout the Middle East, in Greece (the "shoes" see earlier) and on the island of Crete. Greece was an integral part of the Ottoman Empire for quite a while (from the 16th to the 19th Century) during which time it absorbed many Turkish dishes into its National cuisine as was also the case for many other occupied Balkan countries.

2. **Sultan's Delight** - I have been to Turkey more times than I can remember, it is such a spectacular country. A place with a history going back into antiquity; not always that liberal it has to be said. The soldiers of the Ottoman Empire were conquerors with scant regard for the people they subdued. They and their leaders were in the business of power, glory and wealth creation. The dish, "Sultan's delight" or locally "hunkar begendi" also has a pretty long history probably going back to the 17th Century. At this time and over the subsequent centuries the dish was associated with well to do Ottomans in high places, senior administrators and military leaders. There are various recipes that come under the label of "Sultan's delight" but the most extravagant dish that I have to say is a complete delight. It involves a thyme and oregano infused lamb tomato and onion stew, a mixture of pulped aubergine and melted cheese and a bed of boiled white rice Place the rice on a large serving plate, top with the hot, melted cheese and cooked aubergine and finally ladle on the meaty stew. Make sure you have plenty bread on the side, then you have before you a delightful dish fit for a Sultan. Even if you don't have a Sultan at hand, the meal is a joy for anyone privileged enough to have it cooked for them.

3. **Woman's Thighs** - we are not talking about some weird voyeur thing or some weight loss procedure but a delightful plate of traditional lamb koftes. It is well known that koftes, in one form or another, are an important comfort and "feel good" food. You get them throughout the Balkans, Middle East and Gulf States

also anywhere else you might imagine. Indeed they have become an Internationally recognized restaurant dish but also in many countries koftes or koftas are take away favourites or barbeque alternatives to the ubiquitous sausages. Koftes came into being in Turkey and the Arab world (most likely via Iran). Originally they were rounded and then became elongated cigar-shaped savoury mince creations. The rounded version was the predecessor of the meatball that now is an integral part of numerous cuisines around the globe. It has to be a shock to many that neither USA nor Italy had anything at all to do with the invention of meatballs. The other country renowned for their meatball dish is Sweden and their involvement came directly from Turkey via King Charles XII who spent time in the Middle East before returning home. All right meatballs, round koftes, elongated koftas and the whole gang are all over the place, you can find them on any street corner. However only in Turkey is a specific type of kofte called "women's thighs" or locally "kadinbuda kofte". "Women's thighs" in Turkey consist of lamb mince, cooked rice and chopped onion that you mix together and mold into a number of oval patties (preferably thigh shaped?).

4. **The priest's stew** - our Turkish Imams do like their food especially when they are not fainting (see earlier). In addition Greek priests quite like the option of gobbling up a nourishing stew full of booze. It is said the alcohol was at one time a key constituent of this present dish, "the priest's stew". In times not so long past, alcohol and religion were not best of friends but they were not total

enemies. Non-the-less I have the suspicion, without any real proof, that during these transitional times a priest with an interest in alcohol might hide his enthusiasm for the booze from his flock by enjoying a wine-rich stew rather than gulp down a bottle of alcohol in full view? A number of experts believe the dish is of Greek origin and adopted by Turkey minus the wine part. Thus the "priest's stew" became a tea total affair in the Middle East, the alcohol having been replaced by water and a little vinegar. As a result anyone in Turkey can enjoy this extremely tasty dish. The proper name for the stew is "Papaz yahnisi" which is a tasty garlic-rich combination of beef chunks (or lamb on occasion) and whole baby onions slow cooked. The main spices mostly used include different combinations of pepper, plenty cumin, some allspice, cardamom seeds and a little cinnamon. In Turkey I have had the dish only once as lamb because usually it is beef. The recipe always aims for there to be a pleasant vinegary kick in the gravy to counteract the sweetness of the onions.

MIDDLE EAST

1. **Upside Down** - upside down dishes have been around for hundreds of years. Basically it is a way of cooking over the kitchen fire within a high-sided, heavy frying pan. Clearly the heat is fierce at the base but gentler further up. As a result the juicy part of the dish that needs more cooking is best at the bottom of the pot while the more problematic constituents are subjected to relatively milder heat by being above. At the end of cooking, the upside down dish is flipped over so that the topping is served right side upwards. In Western cuisine examples of this approach to cooking are "pineapple upside down cake" a USA staple and the French apple and pastry classic "tarte tatin". In modern times at least it is a means of making nice cakes and puddings whereas our "upside down" is rather unusual being a savoury dish with varied content that is enjoyed all over the Middle East. I think of "maqluba" as a Palestinian special since it is one of their National dishes. Essentially it is well-oiled meat, mixed vegetables, including broken up cauliflower, chopped potatoes and sliced aubergine is next and rice on top. There is also a requirement for a thorough dowsing of the dish with stock. Loads of

aromatic spices such as turmeric, allspice, cardamom and any herbs handy go in the pot also. Then when cooked the whole thing is turned "upside down" with meat on top and place on the table for sharing. Plenty of local salad and salted yoghurt are essential on the side. I like spicy chicken strips mixed in with tomato as the best bottom layer but lamb and onion is also really decent. The well-cooked meat comes out slightly charred and caramelized creating an almost barbeque-like flavour.

2. **Spoiled Daddy** - the Middle East is famous for its tasty dips that can be used with the myriad of types of flat breads these counties produce. The "spoiled daddy" dip is a Lebanese smoked aubergine classic known throughout the World as "baba ganoush". It, like "hummus", is an International specialty that has travelled far and wide. I've even eaten this dip on the American side of the Tex/Mex border with freshly made "tacos", on Orchard Road in Singapore on top of "melba toasts" (they actually called their dip "baba ganoush" didn't taste much like it though) and in Oman it was served up with pitta breads (brilliant). None of these places acknowledged the Lebanese connection to the tasty dip they liked to serve. Personally I find it is such a shame that Lebanon, outside the Arab World, gets little if any credit for the creation of many fabulous dishes. This little country has a claim on being the original home of "hummus". An unlikely claim as it happens but there are many other foods that originated their such as the bread containing salad "fattoush" eaten

everywhere these days. I love their "kibbeh that to me are like exotic "Scotch eggs". Or how about Lebanese "pilaf" that mixes pasta in with the rice? However back to their "baba ganoush". The key thing is to roast the aubergines on a gas hob or barbeque. Mix the rough pulp with tahini paste, lemon juice, olive oil, some spices and liberal salt seasoning and you have your dip. A flourish of pomegranate seeds scattered on top is a pleasant garnish and eat with roasted pitta.

3. **Floaters** - these little balls of deliciousness are a great treat in Syria, which may well be the home of these little fellas. On the other hand they are to be found throughout the Middle East, North Africa and the Gulf States. In some places they are small while in others they are bigger being more than bite sized. The "floaters" or in Arabic "awameh" can be smooth and shiny or coated with sesame seeds and therefore look more mat. These dumpling-like treats have a host of different names in the many places around the Mediterranean where they are eaten. However in all cases they are excruciatingly sweet and deliciously compulsive! Set them alongside a pot of strong and bitter Arabic coffee for balance then they become even more irresistible. In Syria the small dough balls are soaked in honey or sugar syrup while lemon juice and cinnamon bring added taste (as far as I'm concerned cinnamon is a tip-top spice). The balls are deep-fried and while cooking they remain on the surface of the oil hence the name "floaters". Think of "doughnuts" because they also cook on the surface of the oil and need to be flipped over during the cooking process. Perhaps if they were ours we

would have called "awameh" something like "mininuts" perhaps? On the other hand if "doughnuts" were Syrian they might have been known as the "massive floaters". Just a fanciful thought!

4. **Soak** - Iraq and other Middle Eastern countries pool so many of their National dishes. Sometimes the dishes are remarkably similar from place to place while with others they become considerably modified to suit diverse tastes. "Soak" or "tashreeb" is a distinctly Iraqi contribution to the common pool and this rich soup/stew comes in multiple guises in its home country. Therefore its not surprising it varies considerably in constituents, taste and density (from soup to thick stew) throughout the whole Middle Eastern region and beyond. It started life in Iraq as an economy-type of meal sustaining the poor (more euphemistically described by chefs and food writers as peasant food). Thereafter the tasty soups, made up of whatever was available, became widely popular comfort fare so they evolved, in the hands of chefs and amateur cooks into a richer family of stews. The common feature and why I am attracted to this group of meals, is that there is a layer of bread in the communal serving dish or individual bowl. If I have soup or stew in front of me I am a compulsive bread dunker so this Iraqi classic really appeals. Essentially "soak" is chunks of red meat or chicken sealed off and cooked in stock with onions, potatoes, tomatoes and chickpeas. The dish is spiced with cumin, coriander and turmeric. Pour the cooked end product on a bed of torn up flat breads. Enjoy with either spoon or fork.

IRAN

1. **Water Meat** - what could that be, fish, seafood or even hippo or crocodile? No we are in the land of exquisite rice dishes and thee most perfect stews ever created. Our dish is a stew called "abgoosht" breaks down to "ab" for water and "goosht" a word for meat. I suppose irrespective whether if it is fancy or simple "ab" plus "goosht" and a few other odds and sods is the basis of every stew or casserole. I believe Persian cuisine is often not appreciated internationally as a historical powerhouse of food creativity that certainly it has been. Out of Persia went dishes like "byriani" to the Indian subcontinent also the well known "korma curry" followed by much the same route East. When rice came to Persia they made innumerable different preparation approaches such as "polow" that became "pilaf" in countries further west. The Persian enthusiasm for stews was infectious and spread even beyond neighbouring lands to the whole World. Our "abgoosht" is a stew sometimes called "dizi" after the pots the dish was once (and still are) served up in. The "dizi" pots can be very colourful so they are sold in the Iranian markets both as utensils and as ornaments. The meat (lamb or beef)

is cooked with onions, tomatoes, chickpeas, beans, potatoes and dried limes. Characteristically the broth is eaten with chunks of bread separately from the solid meat and vegetables. Hence the "water" and "meat" are two separate courses.

2. **Bottom of the Pot** - who on earth wants to eat the base of some old pot? Well I'm sure you have gathered that it isn't literally the "bottom of the pot" but "tahdig", as it is called in Persian, is the food packed in at the very base that gets the most heat over the fire when being cooked. The foods of particular interest are the bounty of savoury rice dishes that Persian cuisine are renowned for. Upwards in the pot the rice just cooks but at the bottom it gets crispy. Rice dishes such as "pilaf" (classic savoury rice throughout the Middle East), "byriani" (actually a Persian creation that went to India rather than the other way around) and "estanboli polo" (a rice, vegetable and meat stew) develop a touch of "tahdig" with slow cooking but its not the major objective in preparing these dishes. Outdoor cooking of a "paella" over a big fire, with minimum disruption of the rice creates crusty bits on the bottom that are prized by "paella" lovers. In Iran however we take rice crusty bits to another level in for example the meat stuffed rice cake called "tahchin" and the New Year special rice "morasa polo". They in terms of crust are not top of the heap that award goes to the rice dish that is simply called "bottom of the pot". The whole exercise is to create as much "tahdig" as possible and so the rice dish itself is called "tahdig" or "chelo ba tahdig". The trick is to get plenty

of oil or ghee (clarified butter) at the bottom of your pot so while the basmati long grain rice above is steamed the bottom stuff is fried. Others swear by having a layer of bread between the pot base and the "tahdig" forming rice or even (if inclined) a layer of potatoes. In addition there are enthusiasts who like plenty of yoghurt in the bottom rice. Saffron water or turmeric powder can be used as colouring so when the rice cake is turned out upside down on the plate the yellow rice has a thick orange crust on top. See also the other way round for "upside down" under Middle East earlier.

3. **Fried Herbs** - a Scots friend of mine who has an Iranian wife invited me over for dinner. No it wasn't to anywhere extremely exotic; it was the outskirts of Warrington in Cheshire. My pal was extremely excited about what we were to eat and told me it was beloved in Iran and called "ghormeh sabzi." I go back a bit, well much more than a bit. This was a time when the mobile phone was walking to another telephone box because the first was out of order! Also the internet was the space between two fishing boats. I'm sure only some of you will appreciate what I'm taking about and none of you are young? Any way curiosity got the better of me and I found a literal translation of "ghormeh" and "sabzi" as "fried herbs". Did sound a bit green even for me who had two vegetarian children and a carnivore to cook for each weekend. What I did find out when I got to Warrington and stopped looking at dictionaries was that "fried herbs" transforms into "king of stews" an Iranian National dish. It is a lamb or beef special

cooked in a cornucopia of greens that include spinach, spring onions, parsley, coriander, anything else green and fenugreek (not too common in the UK but all over the Middle East). Also kidney beans and dried limes enhance the dish. Gorgeous!

4. **Slamming** - doesn't sound that appetizing but now we have left the world of Persian stews and entered the world of the Persian's second love, the "kabob" that elsewhere would be known as the "kebab". Some believe the "kebab" was introduced to Persia from elsewhere but the dish without doubt has its soul in Iran. By way of comparison, the hamburger originated in Germany but it did not become a burger in a bun until it reached the shores of America. Who would doubt that this fast food or tasty meal owes its allegiance to the USA? Personally whether you call it a "kabob" or a "kebab" the same holds true for Persian cuisine and that is where it belongs. Equally in the same way there a gazillion different burgers there are also as many different types of "kebab." Often they arose in the creative heartland of Persia. Our "slamming" is a type of "kebab" that in Iran is called "kabob koobideh" - does not trip off the tongue admittedly but we all know it well! The "kkobideh" is the word for "slamming" because the meat (usually lamb but can be others) is slammed to mince by a mallet on a flat stone. The meat is mixed with onion, mint, spices and wrapped around a metal skewer. Flat metal skewers are far more popular in Persian cooking than the round wooded versions used throughout the rest of the Middle East and for

that matter far and wide. The metal skewer used for cooking the "slamming kebab" is known in parts of Iran as a "seekh". Of course we are talking about a common starter in an Indian restaurant, street food nearly everywhere and a takeaway special. Of course we are talking about "seekh kebab" that has a much better known cousin we all know as "shish kebab".

ARABIAN PENINSULA

1. **Dew** - sadly these days Yemen in country terms is the epitome of all that is impoverished, subjugated and oppressed in this rather cruel World we live in. Unfortunately, unlike its wealthy neighbours, Yemen has no oil reserves so has little influence in these days when money matters. Their economy is not helped by protracted civil war. On the other hand historical Yemen was the home of the legendary Queen of Sheeba. I am indifferent to tea but a coffee addict so I know Yemen is the original home of the drink. If you are enjoying a mocha with friends remember that is the name of Yemen's major port. A substantial dish from Yemen is sometimes called "haneeth" but also known as "mandi" that happens, I am told, to be derived from the Arabic word for dew, "nada". Traditionally the meat, treated with a heady mix of cumin and cardamom-rich Yemeni spice mix, is placed in a sealed pot and buried underground for a few hours on hot coals. The slow cooked meat, often lamb or chicken, is served up on rice topped with dried fruit and nuts. The glistening droplets on the meat when served up is thought to remind the diner of dew - hence the name?

2. **Pressed** - rather a strange name for a dish but that is the literal translation of "kabsa" from Arabic to English. "Kabsa" is eaten everywhere in the Arabian Peninsula and the Middle East but nowhere more so than Saudi Arabia where the dish is a National treasure. Of course the Kingdom is by far the largest country in the Peninsula and dominates the region in many ways including cuisine. I understood the meat in "kabsa" was chicken pieces usually with skin on and well seasoned with spices. It turns out that my assumption was wrong having been told it could be made with fish and all sorts of meats including lamb, goat and even on occasion some camel. Your choice of meat, along with abundant rice, is cooked in a rich, spicy gravy. The gravy contains onion and plenty tomato and it is favoured with a spice mixture that is a combination of saffron, cardamom, coriander, cloves, chilli flakes, cumin, pepper and dried limes ("lumi"). The limes give the gravy a tang while the chilli gives it a pronounced kick. The meat is cooked in the gravy first then removed and the rice has its turn. When ready the meat is "pressed" back in. Serve up on a large plate for communal use then finish off with nuts, fresh coriander and fresh lime segments. Plenty of salad on the side embellishes the "kabsa" as does yoghurt and flatbreads.

3. **Hit** - the dish is actually called "madrouba" and it is a specialty in a number of Gulf States, including Qatar, The Emirates, Bahrain although it is loved the most by Omanis (at least that's what they told me in the capital Muscat). It is quite a special dish that is totally

flavoursome. Definitely a treat that often has pride of place at special events. However because it takes quite long to prepare it is not on the menu of your usual lunch-time café in Muscat or anywhere else along the Gulf for that matter. It is much more a dish that you might have at home for a family gathering or, something that might be present at a celebration or some such gathering of like-minded folks. Not that much of that happened during those bleak COVID times when I wrote this book. Essentially "madrouba" is chicken (when I've had it) or other meat cooked with rice, vegetables (like onions, tomatoes and peppers), dried limes (an Omani addition) plus lots of coriander and local spices. All the ingredients are cooked together in a big pot. When ready, the contents of the pot are given such a pounding with a big wooden spoon (in other words they are "hit") until we have a uniform mush. Now that doesn't sound attractive, nor does it look all that clever even on a well laid out table. I gave a lecture in Oman and afterwards there was a feast that had "madruba" as one of the dishes. I didn't take to its looks but my hosts were insistent I try some. I'm glad they did because believe me it tastes heavenly!

4. **Disc of Rope** - now a "disc of rope" does not sound too inviting as a treat to me but that is the literal translation of "gers ogaily". I understand that "gers" in English is a disc of something while "ogaily" is a derivative of "ogal", a kind of rope like structure. It turns out the "ogal" is no ordinary rope but the black fabric or woven hair band that goes twice around the head to hold the

Arab headdress in place. In Kuwait, our "disc of rope" is a cake with a wonderful smell. So prominent and distinctive was the aroma given off by the Kuwaiti cake that it was also known locally as the perfume cake. Now I can boast to having eaten "disk of rope" in its home setting but admit to being in the home setting for only a few days. I intended to be there longer but it was July 1990. Less than two weeks later Iraq invaded and the first Gulf War thereafter was imminent. I was out of that stricken country with not too many days to spare. Mind you I still remember an afternoon with cake and strong coffee. The cake had been made in a wide but flat bunt tin so it looked like a giant polo mint-shaped sponge. There was no mint flavour or smell. The taste, colour and perfume were down to the cake being cooked with plenty saffron, cardamom, rose water and sesame seeds on top. Unusual, very regional but best mates with strong coffee.

NORTH AFRICA

1. **Local Life** - back in the early 1990s I worked for a while in the Delta Region of Northern Egypt. My flat looked out over the Nile, sounds fantastic except for the biting flies and mosquitoes that shared the flat and but not the rent. Despite the bitey stinging things buzzing around, my flat was homely and my landlord like clockwork made sure I had warm bread every morning. I can't emphasize enough how important bread happens to be to the Egyptian way of living. So to describe a local variety of bread as being "life" itself is not any kind of exaggeration from an Egyptian's point of view. It is eaten at every meal and numerous types of bread are used to scoop up food in preference to using a knife and fork. "Local Life" ["Eish (life) Baladi (local or traditional)"] is a yeast containing bread cooked, like all Egyptian breads, in an extremely hot wood-burning oven. Our bread is made from strong whole meal flour that comes out of the heat as a kind of small but rather thick "pitta" ideal for tearing up and dipping into sauces of various types or holding onto lumps of meat, fish or vegetables captured from a stew. Egyptian breads are full of flavour after all the birthplace of bread was

Egypt way back perhaps as much as 5,000 years! If you take an Egyptian flatbread cut it in half, make a pocket, add a little chopped salad with lime juice, stuff in "falafels" (another Egyptian invention), top with a "tahini dressing" and more lime, you have the perfect sandwich.

2. **Shaken** - on this occasion it is not anything to do with a James Bond drink. If you remember "Shaken not stirred" is Bond's famous demand when ordering a vodka martini. Our present dish originated in its current form in Tunisia where it is called "shakshouka" and in that country translates to somewhere between "shaken" and "all mixed up". Essentially the dish is a full to overflowing frying pan of chopped vegetables, including onions, red peppers, crushed garlic with a rich tomato base that is thickened up in the hot pan with chilli, coriander, cumin and paprika. This fairly hot, brilliantly red and fiery sauce is the cauldron that serves to cook eggs and once they are prepared the dish is ready. It makes a great lunch or a really zingy breakfast. Now if you have been to Spain, Mexico or numerous other nations you might have eaten something very similar? Indeed Tunisia may have got their dish from their Sephardic Jewish minority who of course came to Tunisia from Spain. In turn Tunisian Jewish peoples in later years settled in Israel and the Spanish/ Tunisian egg and tomato special had a new set of admirers. It can be very, very fiery (Mexico), it can be incredibly tasty (Spain and Tunisia) and it can be both (Israel). It you

have never eaten this well travelled dish then it is time to have a go - so treat yourself its time to be "shaken".

3. **Velvet Soup** - there is a remarkably exotic looking cake in the USA called red velvet cake that, apart from our soup, are the only foods called velvet that I know. Our soup has nothing to do with the USA but it is very much at home in the Maghreb of North Africa and more specifically the countries of Algeria and Morocco. It is reputed that "harira" is the number one soup in Morocco but I have been told many times that "velvet soup" came into being in Algeria. Why velvet? Well the soup has a glistening or velvety sheen when served out. The Arab word "hareer" equates to velvetiness when translated into English. The soup is eaten at any time of the year but it is associated with "breaking the fast" at Ramadan being nutritious and tasty. It is a lamb-based (or even chicken-based) soup with vegetables, lentils and spices like "ras el hanout". The Algerian version of "harira" is usually less complicated than its Moroccan sibling but the soups have more in common with each other than differences. Some Italian friends and I set off from Marrakesh in a sturdy vehicle and went some way into the dessert crossing over into Algeria. Dessert nights are as freezing as the day is hot - one of my thoughtful companions had brought a huge vat of "harira" so there we were committing two crimes. Enjoying the Moroccan copy of an Algerian soup in the land of its origin and not having any right to be in Algeria in the first place!

4. **Gazelle's Horns** - it does seem to me that North Africans have in general a rather sweet tooth and that applies to Moroccans in particular. Suits me down to the ground although I remember spending one New Year's Eve in Morocco and wasn't sure if I was drunk from the sugar overload or from the alcohol. Either way I celebrated New Year in style and was fit for nothing the next day. A rather peculiar hangover with rather less of an after taste of wine and whisky but more of marzipan and orange blossom water! That is some admission from a Scotsman abroad! Of the many pastry fancies that are found everywhere in Morocco, one I like the most of all is "kaab el ghzal". These very sweet orange soaked pastries are special treats that typically are packed to overflowing with a delicious filling made from sugar, almond paste and cinnamon stirred into orange blossom water. The unusual concoction is placed on pastry circles that are folded over and crimped closed. The crescent-shaped delights are cooked ready for eating. Alternatively in some places the cooked pastries thereafter are dipped in sugar or honey or get a coating of crushed nuts. These little guys are not restricted to Morocco but you can find them all over North Africa though they may not be called gazelle's horns. One confusion I have not sorted out is it appears the exact literal translation of "kaab el ghzal" is "gazelle's ankles" and not exactly "gazelle's horns" as they are referred to in English. Indeed Kaab is a common male personal name in the Arab World. Whether the pastries are compared to horns, ankles or what ever doesn't matter much since they are truly exceptional sweet eating.

AFRICA ELSEWHERE

1. **Walky Talky** - is a meal that originated in the South African townships where everything needs to be eaten up. No one is rich enough for there to be much in the way of waste food or waste anything. It is fair to say the "walky talky" dish is not particularly appetizing to Western sensitivities but it is perfectly nutritious. The meal consists of chicken feet (walky) and heads (talky) in the one dish boiled or battered and deep-fried. Now chicken head eating is a bit extreme I agree, although fried heads go down well in Indonesia and in Thailand where they are roasted on a stick over an open fire. Always eat the brains I'm told, mind you at only 3 grams or 0.1 ounces it is hardly a feast. On the other hand, the feet are enjoyed all over the World from South East Asia to South America. In China they are a banquet delicacy, nicely spiced they taste all right but personally I can't get as enthusiastic about crunching away at a foot, in quite the way my Chinese friends seem to relish. In these days of mobile phones, you might think the "walky talky" is on its way out? That does not seem to be the case because there is still a role for them in factories and building sites where your mobile

is less than ideal. The "walky talky", or more correctly the two-way transponder, was invented in the 1930s and came into its own during WWII. The original devices weighed over 5 pounds and were a foot and a half tall. The "walky talky" is still a great hit as a children's toy. Great fun was had with our childhood knocked together version consisting of two empty tin cans connected by a length of string. One of us would shout "can you hear me?" and the inevitable reply being "What?"

2. **Zanzibar Pizza** - just sounds like a rather exotic pizza with some special African toppings you would think? Except, as it turns out, a "Zanzibar pizza" is geographically reasonably accurate in name at least but food wise there is no pizza anywhere in the World including those centres of pizza innovation, Italy and the USA, that produces anything like the Zanzibar creation. Creation is the wrong word because there are a plethora of creations. You can throw almost anything into a "Zanzibar pizza" - rather like a typical American pizza menu with knobs on. It is based on a simple pancake-like mixture, spread out as thin as possible and cooked in gee (clarified butter). Then on goes a shovel of fillings that can be anything your heart (or stomach) desires. The pancake and filling is folded over rather roughly and there you have it ready to eat best you can manage. Eating this construction is not an easy process but that is part of the fun. A few examples of popular fillings give you a sense of what you might be in for. Mince in various forms with chilli is common and would go alongside processed cheese or cream

cheese. Mayonnaise seems to be everywhere in these creations as are piles of vegetables and fruit like avocado (with extra mayo and hot sauce). Sweet versions favour "Nutella" and mango sauce and they often live in your "Zanzibar pizza" mixed up together! Sweet or savoury, no combinations of unlikely bedfellows are off limits in the construction of your designer "Zanzibar pizza".

3. **Rolex** - you really need to "watch" this East African, Ugandan delicacy! Sorry I could not resist writing that it is a naff statement but totally irresistible thing to say. All my life I have wanted to have a Rolex Oyster watch but it has never quite happened. Whenever I had the savings, believe me that was never often, something happed so there was always competition for the savings that was always more sensible and practical than my Swizz timepiece intentions. I once got a Singapore special that was cheap as chips, the weight was completely wrong but at a distance it was passible (only just). I wore in now and then but lost it at a driving range in Essex. A wild swing, the thing flew off my wrist and hit some poor soul in the next bay. Don't know what was more embarrassing, apologizing profusely to the injured man or picking up the remnants of the fake Rolex. Now in Uganda there is a kind of fake Rolex also but this is an edible one. Fake because there is not too much Ugandan in this Uganda breakfast special. The wrap is chapatti dough of Indian extraction while the contents are invariably egg but mixed with chopped tomato, onion, coriander and other bits and pieces (from everywhere). The eggs and the rest of the filling is put into the

chapatti as it cooks then rolled. Up until the 1970s there was a sizable Indian population in Uganda approaching 100,000 but the dictator *Idi Amin* expelled most of them. However their influence on Uganda society was profound even down to some of the foods enjoyed in that troubled country. Rolex is street food and working folks breakfast or for that matter to be eaten any time of the day. Nothing about a Rolex is traditional Ugandan but the combination of ingredients and enthusiasm for the wrap (roll in Rolex) is an Indian legacy within that East African country (there is still an Indian population today but much depleted).

4. **Pepper Soup** - now in Europe or the Americas, pepper soup would be a nice sweet vegetable creation, full of flavour but mild. However we are in a different continent and the concept of pepper is quite different we jump from a sweet capsicum to an old name for spices including pretty hot ones especially if you want to make African pepper soup. The tasty brew is eaten throughout West Africa but Nigeria appears to be its home. Only in one sense is the name "pepper soup" a bit weird and that is we now use the word pepper to describe a complex combination of spices and condiments. Way in the past pepper was the catchall name that was applied to any spices. The rhyme "Peter Piper picked a peck of pickled peppers" for example is about nefarious goings on of countries wanting to muscle in on the spice trade. Our Nigerian "pepper soup" is a fiery creation whereby a meaty stock is infused with a varied and bountiful mixtures of spices many very African others not. The

soup is a rich carnivore stew that can be beef, offal, goat, chicken or whatever else happens to be handy. The dish contains local aromatic leaves while the spices differ from place to place but chill powder, scotch bonnet peppers, ginger, black pepper and cayenne pepper usually play a part giving the finished product quite a fierce kick. Nigerians do like their spices (peppers) whether locally foraged or from far away lands. A distant relative we called Uncle Richard had once headed the Lagos port authority in the turbulent 1960/70s and said one of his better memories was the vivid and contrasting colours of the sacks of spices offloaded at the busy, chaotic dockside. The sacs and other containers were legion so the smell of rich spice must have been overpowering - in an otherwise smelly dock no bad thing I should imagine!

THE STANS

1. **Half Moon** - there are versions of this dish in many adjacent countries but it is only in Turkmenistan is it called "half moon" or more correctly "gutap". The food is a flatbread filled with lamb and onions or beef and potato. Other fillings include spinach, even pumpkin of various types and other vegetables. The "gutlap" is folded over and the filling sealed in so you have your "half moon" shape before cooking in a pan on top of the stove or even an open fire if necessary. Turkmenistan was part of the Soviet Union until 1991 but independence has only lead to extreme oppression and it is effectively a closed country. Although its modern history is rather torrid, the region has a colourful past being on the spice trades routes and also a land of horses. In the territory as it is today to the west Turkmenistan borders the Caspian Sea but much of this large land is dessert and mountains. It has dishes novel to that country but many recipes have spilled over to be shared with its neighbours and of course that exchange also works the other way round. "Half moons" are one of Turkmenistan's food gifts to most of Central Asia. "Gutlab" is very much a tasty convenience food eaten by hand when required

rather than part of some more formal meal. As such it is suited to this area, and Turkmenistan in particular, for historically we are dealing with a population of horsemen who, with their women and children, were used to packing their belongings and moving on. Of course the modern population is no longer nomadic but "half moon" dates back to a time when they were much more mobile than today.

2. **Stretch the Dough** - for this dish we go next door from Turkmenistan to the lands of Uzbekistan. I have to say like its neighbour it is not one of the best-known spots in the World today. In modern times it was absorbed into the communist USSR but even when it became once again a country in its own right it has descended to being an autocratic police state. A not uncommon fate for emerging nations in Central Asia. Yet once Uzbekistan blossomed such that cities like ancient Samarkand, on the one time Silk Road liking China to the West, were legendary places. Also that city was one of the powerhouses for the ruthless Tamerlane and his vast warrior hoards. Situated between West and East, Uzbekistan over the centuries has had numerous influences on their cuisine. One being that pasta plays an important role in the Uzbek diet up to modern (and not so modern) times coming originally from the east (China) rather than west (Italy and the rest). Our "stretch the dough" dish is a pasta the Uzbeks called "lagman" derived from a local word "lyumyan" that translates to "stretch the dough". By doing so you are on your way to making homemade pasta noodles that are

extremely good fried up with spices, tomato and onions. The big stretched pasta also serves as a key ingredient in soups and a host of other dishes including stir-fries. One soup, is so closely associated with "stretch the dough" noodles, it is called "lagman soup" in Uzbekistan and other countries. It consists of various types of meat, potatoes, carrots, onion, peppers and other veg flavoured with coriander, garlic and cumin all on a base of our favourite Uzbek noodles.

3. **Five Fingers** - no you are not meant to eat some ones fingers so we can move on from there. The dish traditionally is considered to be Kasakhstan's National dish though it is also very popular in next-door Kyrgyzstan. Locally known as "Beshbarmak", it is often made in the home kitchen but it has a very long history as a celebration dish for banquets and the like. It has earned a certain amount of kudos in its homelands. "Beshbarmak" is a special dish to be treated in a respectful way to honour both the hosts and the dish itself. Therefore diners and guests often drop into historical and cultural authenticity by abandoning modern day cutlery and using a single hand. That hand of course has "five fingers" to grasp some food from the communal dish. Collective eating in this manner is Worldwide including elsewhere in Central Asia, throughout the Middle East, all of the Gulf States, many parts of Africa and of course India. We Western Europeans are not that all together with sharing plates involving lots of fingers - mind you there is always the KFC bucket special and the grab while you can slices

of a giant pizza. I have done the family share thing in various places around the World. Sometimes it's tough when you and some ones Grannie are passing to each other handfuls of slimy delights (I'm thinking of an okra stew I shared in the Middle East) and God knows what else from the bowl. Other times around a fire on a starry, starry night when everyone shares a classic dish of BBQ ribs. All the diners become really close during that kind of meal and for that moment fingers rule ok!

4. **Melt in the Mouth** - it is hard to imagine in conflict stricken Afghanistan, worse every day, that there is any normal family life within that country. It just happens that Afghan people conduct the usual everyday pursuits and do the ordinary things that families do all over the World. Big extended families they are too. I have read that the average family size in Afghanistan is between seven and eight people with three or four generations sharing the same space that might be just a few rooms. Afghans are by no means unique in this extended family arrangement since that would apply to all the countries of Central Asia and beyond into parts of the Middle East and the Indian Subcontinent. Of course establishing large extended family units makes all sorts of economic sense, especially where grown up children can't afford to set up home on their own away from the parental umbrella. However an equally important driver is the very strong family bonds that exist in countries like Afghanistan reinforced to some extent by collective meals. Flatbreads cooked in clay ovens are an Afghan staple. There is a love of roasts but these are luxury items

for many. Pies, stews and pilafs figure prominently as do sweet pastries and cakes. Many love an Afghanistan biscuit called "ab e dandon" and its name translates to what I understand is "water of the teeth". That translation makes no sense at all literally but it seems to mean "melt in the mouth". The "melt in the mouth" biscuit is made from well-kneaded dough consisting of flour, light sugar, ground cardamom and rose water. Scattered on top is more sugar and usually crushed pistachios. Butter is rarely used in Afgan baking, it is just too expensive and hard to get anywhere, so vegetable oil is the usual option. Afghans pride themselves on their hospitality so visitors would be refreshed with local tea and "ab e dandon" biscuits.

INDIAN SUBCONTINENT

1. **Katakat** - is a much loved dish from Pakistan that originated somewhere in the Karachi area. The word "katakat" in not a word as such but the noise made by a chef in a kitchen cooking meat rediculously quickly on a very hot plate. A cooking technique where you maneuver the food around as rapidly as you can so it cooks but does not burn and the chef's utensils make the noise "kata kata kata kat"! It is much like stir fry without the wok to help you out. So the name of our dish is like "boom- boom- boom" of a drum or "rat-a-tat-tat" of a machine gun or even "sizzle- sizzle" the sound of food cooking. The figure of speech I think is onomatopoeia and the name of our dish is one of those. City versions of the dish, particularly in Karachi, are often fish-based but elsewhere in Pakistan it is well-spiced offal. Definitely "katakat" can turn out to be an offal overdrive and so therefore challenging to our British eating sensitivies. For example a "katakat" might consist of fine chopped, flash fried, goat meat, spicy liver, testicles, kidney, heart and for good measure, chopped brains. Irrespective of the meats, offal or even fish that are central to the dish, your "katakat" is best served as a manageable portion

in the middle of a "roti" (unleavened flatbread) and topped with a range of chutneys to add to the spicy edge of the dish.

2. **Bombay Duck** - Bombay changed its name to Mumbai in the mid 1990s for a number of reasons including the fact that the British chose Bombay as the city's name back in old colonial times so better to have something more appropriate to India. Even so many residents, out of habit, still refer to their city as Bombay. It is India's largest city with a population at the time of writing that is well in excess of twenty million. Mumbai is the financial heart of India and also it is a large busy port, the largest on the west coast. The thriving film industry still refers to itself as Bollywood (not Mullywood as yet!) Equally our "Bombay duck" dish retains its colonial identity. Duck is my favourite meat but the Bombay version isn't duck, it is made from a repulsively ugly fish with a face and toothy mouth that would be at home in a horror movie. This lizardfish does not become any the more endearing when it is out of water because the fish stinks a bit, rather a lot actually! The problem is that "Bombay duck" appears as a glut for the fishermen at the start of the rainy season so far more of the fish is landed than can be eaten fresh. As a result it is smoked, dried and cured for sale locally or elsewhere adding exponentially to the stink. Thus, smell aside, "Bombay duck" is a dish in its own right though more often serving as a flavouring or even a condiment. Why the name? One story states that in the time of the British Raj mail trains were ideal for transporting our wiffy

dried fish (no people on board) all over the country from Bombay. These smelly trains were known as "Bombay dak" (where "dak" is the word for mail) therefore just a step away from "Bombay duck". Having seen this fish close up, I cant help thinking it must have been a very brave or incredibly desperate hero who looked it up and down and was the first to eat it!

3. **Jumping Potatoes** - there are all sorts of potato options in the World at large but jumping ones are unusual no matter what country they are from. Really I think of India as a place of limited potato eating; rice and unleavened breads certainly, but spuds are definitely not all that prominent. Then, I remember the ever-popular "Bombay potatoes," how about "potato samosas", "potato pakoras", a plethora of "potato curries" and "potato snacks"? It turns out there are a surprising abundance of Indian subcontinent dishes involving, or based around, the potato ("aloo a lot" you might not say). Now I'm not claiming "jumping potatoes" are a common Indian food but the name makes them an interesting one. In fact by all accounts "jumping potatoes" is a festival side dish associated with a small Jewish community in India sadly in decline these days. It consists of peeled potatoes boiled in salted water rich in turmeric. They are cooked for a very short time just to yellow them and then they are drained. After that the potatoes go into a deep fryer for a while to soften but not crisp. At this point the cook lets the potato cool in the oil. Before serving your potatoes need a very hot blast in oil to go crisp and brownish turmeric yellow. I

guess with the in and out of water and oil there will be a fair amount of jumping going on and splashing too no doubt. These crispy "aloo makala" ("fried potato") I'm told still jump from the plate to your lap if you fork them too much - hence the nickname.

4. **Vinegar Curry** - sounds like a nightmare and it is true you need to really like curries to enjoy this one or should I say this family of dishes that have a number of distinctive characteristics in common, not necessarily shared with the cuisine of the rest of India. They all come from that part of India, once a colony of Portugal, called Goa. The Portuguese brought chillies to Goa from South America and in this part of India they grew like weeds so "Goan curries" are as hot as the fires of hell. Possibly the best known of the vinegar curries is "vindaloo" so loved by drunken Brits on their late Saturday night visit to the curry house. Unlike almost anywhere else in India, Goans (supposedly Christian when under Portuguese Catholic control) rather enjoyed pork so it was the dominant meat for curries in this area for some time. As a result the mutton or chicken vindaloo, so prominent on curry house menus in the UK, is not really the authentic dish. The Portuguese in the past and even now like the sharp tang of vinegar at the base of some of their dishes. Vinegary fish large and small are popular and chicken specialties such as "arroz de cabidela" have a vinegar kick. Although it is pork meals like "vina dosh" that is a heady mix of pork, masses of garlic and red wine vinegar that is most popular with locals. However acidic enthusiasm

reached another level with those Portuguese explorers that travelled here there and everywhere. It is said that Portuguese sailors lived off heavily pickled pork when they were at sea so developed a taste for a vinegar-rich base to their food wherever they happen to establish a colony somewhere in the World. For instance the famous "piri piri sauce" from Mozambique was first created by Portuguese settlers and is heavily flavoured with dark vinegar and lemon juice. Further "Devil's curry" from the Portuguese Malaccans is fiery but has the pronounced tang of vinegar in every mouthful.

THAILAND

1. **Blood Clams** - definitely a seafood horror show. I can see the movie in side my head, the damsel in distress is running around being chased by ginormous vampire clams snapping their shells together in lurid anticipation of an imminent blood meal! Hang on clams are stuck to rocks and don't do a lot of running about. They do move as it happens - I should know, I filmed them by time-lapse photography on rocks by the seashore in Scotland many years ago. Got wet, knew quite a lot about tides, missed several weeks of good boozer time but after all that my little sprinters had progressed a few millimeters. Insights into what you have to sacrifice in life to get a poor quality zoology degree. As it turns out our blood clams or cockles have a haemoglobin-like pigment inside them (the pigment that colours red blood cells) so if you eat the flesh a reddish liquid is released. You can enjoy "hoy kraeng" in Bangkok (or elsewhere in Thailand and South East Asia) by the shovel full (if you want) along with a generous portion of soy plus additional fierce dipping sauces. Though I do point out to those who might be future tourists and backpackers that many of us have been known to

suffer from the "revenge of the clams" so best get fresh ones and go for those that have been through a steamer or simply boiled in salty water. Many are not cooked or only partly cooked before serving and at that point "blood clams" if you are unlucky can become "those bloody clams!"

2. **Galloping Horses** - horses in Thailand, like elsewhere, are raced professionally and used locally for recreation. They are an important part of the Country's vast tourist industry and often horses also are used as working animals. At the time of writing (2021-22), Thai horses are under serious threat from an African virus and in recent years many have succumbed to their infection. On the other hand, our "galloping horses" are a pre-dinner nibble, a rather tasty starter or an interesting side plate at a lavish buffet. The dish consists of a meaty mix on top of sliced fruits that are primarily slices of pineapple but also sometimes orange. Not a horse in sight as it turns out galloping or otherwise. Personally I'm not sure if the meaty mix is a jocky on top of a fruity horse or the meaty top is the horse's head while the fruity bit is the body. From the ones I have seen and greedily swallowed they didn't do any galloping given they have no legs! These nibbles are called in Thai "ma haw." This country is a monarchy and the dish is thought to have been created for a Thai king called Rama VII, from the early 20th Century, who was by all accounts horse-mad and then some. However more likely it is an import from China, via peoples who migrated into the country. The pork mince that forms the ball on top is cooked in

soy sauce, onion, garlic, sugar, coriander and crushed peanuts. Thereafter a savoury pork mince ball is rolled out and placed on sliced pineapple or other fruits that make a suitable base.

3. **Dancing Shrimps** - the dish is known as "goong ten" in Thai and it is very well known and often talked about by locals. Its home territory is throughout Northern Thailand stretching as far south as Bangkok. Our "dancing" delicacy is sought out by a certain type of tourists, for them it is a "must try before leaving the Country". To their way of thinking it is a right of passage requirement. You will not get this dish in a restaurant but it is there on the streets of towns and cities in special food carts and street food stalls. What I am talking about is a green herb (mint, coriander, lemongrass and the like) and onion salad. The salad is drenched with local spices, plenty of fish sauce, more than a fair amount of strong lime juice and plenty of chilli. This fierce, fiery mix is dolloped onto one or two shovel fulls of freshwater prawns often from the Mekong River. At this point it is best if your meal is served in a bowl rather than on a plate and also the bowl should have a lid. The lid is not an affectation but a necessity, especially if you don't wish your supper to "dance" off down the street. "Dancing shrimps" is not some fanciful name pluck out of the air to make the dish sound special but an actual description of the active prawns. The crustaceans are so fresh they are still living. So after being drenched with hot spice and acidic lime juice they are at the very least seriously pissed off and probably in

complete agony I suspect. They writhe (dance) about in the sharp salad but some sort of relief is at hand when finally the prawns are eaten up by a hungry diner (I guess you would need to be fairly ravenous to swallow these sad little wriggly fellows?).

4. **Boat Noodles** - perhaps not such a strange name to you? Although to me when I first heard of them I thought they had to be pasta shaped like a sampan or some sort of other watercraft? We know that Italian pasta shapes are ridiculously varied from cylinders, hair, sheets, bows, spirals, wheels, elbows, ears and even rice-shaped. Chinese and Japanese noodles are mostly elongated but also massively varied in shape, thickness and even colour. However our Thai "boat noodles" turn out not to be the shape of the pasta involved but where you eat them! Way back in the past going back to the Middle ages in this part of the world, meat and noodle dishes were served out from boats on the waterways to customers on the banks. This practice has been going on for century after century but it is less common these days. Non-the-less the "boat noodle" dishes, headed by a stew-like soup, can still be found in Bangkok and elsewhere. If you get a portion of these noodle delicacies they tend to be sold in small "taster" portions. The very rich soup has a beef base infused with killer flavours and of course it is packed with special homemade noodles. This hefty, meat-rich noodle soup is exotic and unusual mostly because it is served from special waterway boats but also traditionally because it is thickened with blood rather than flour or breadcrumbs.

VIETNAM, CAMBODIA AND LAOS

1. **Water Fern Cake** - the dish comes from Vietnam a country still trying to find its way in the World after years of internal strife and the ravages of a brutish war. Vietnam is an old country with traditions going back to times now forgotten while their monarchy has thousands of years of history but destroyed by the French during WWI when the emperor was exiled to Africa after instigating a failed coup against their colonial overlords. Vietnam has a great deal to offer visitors to their rather beautiful country that includes a sophisticated cuisine evolved over centuries but has more recent influences left by the French. For instance you can get French style baguettes everywhere but filled with very Vietnamese fare. Our "water fern cake" does not come from colonial or modern Vietnam but way back in history when they were made as finger food for royalty. The dynastic seat of Vietnamese royalty was a walled city in the middle of the country called Hue. Here the emperor and family lived the good life eating well and enjoying "water fern cakes" or "bahn beo". Essentially "bahn beo" rice cakes

are made now as they were in imperial times. A mixture of rice flour, tapioca flour and water are mixed to form a batter that is steam cooked as flat circles creating the characteristic white cakes. There are various toppings such as a mix of macerated fresh or dried prawns, chopped spring onion tops cooked in oil and vibrant green also fatty pork mince more lard than meat are all popular. Along side might be pickles but there is always Vietnamese dipping sauce. "Bahn beo" may look like "water ferns" to some but not to me although our "water fern cakes" are yummy non-the-less. In recent times they are popular street food commonly found from Da Nang down to Ho Chi Minh City (Saigon).

2. **Fish in the Fire Lake** - The land of Cambodia has had its nightmares in the past, particularly with respect to the murderous Khmer Rouge who took power in the mid 1970s and effectively exterminated nearly two million Cambodians and destroyed much of the Cambodian way of life. The country's academics and middle classes were obliterated, all forms of modern industrial development culled and their cultural heritage was wiped out. People with any kind of skill were held in deep suspicion and death was likely. Mass murder was not restricted to intellectuals people with particular abilities not admired by the Khmer were eliminated. Haute cuisine was decadent cooking so far too many chefs were killed to the extent that the whole of Cambodian classic cuisine was imperiled. It is therefore a delight to discuss a surviving classic Cambodian dish that is a celebration special called rather beautifully

"fish in the fire lake". Two massive bodies of water, teaming with fish, dominate the country. There is the mighty Mekong river and a vast lake, connected to the Mekong, called the Tonle Sap. As a result Cambodians eat a large amount of freshwater fish that they enjoy steamed, stewed or fried. Further a vast quantity of fish is preserved or pickled for later use or just simply to intensify flavour. It turns out that our "fish" might well have come from these huge bodies of water but the "fire lake" has nothing to do with any real river or lake. Our dish is known locally as "trei bung kanh chhet" and there are two key features of this excellent dish basically it is a large, intact fried fish (the fish) on top of a spicy vegetable and coconut curry (the "fire lake"). The curry has a base of coconut milk (unusual for Cambodia but associated with special occasions), more than its fair share of chopped chilli, plenty of yellow "kroeung" (a Cambodian spice paste rich in turmeric) and the vegetables mostly consist of cauliflower and cabbage. The Tonle Sap these days is under threat, climate change and population pressures conspire to cause massive reduction in water levels in recent times. Heat and drought make the "fire lake" not just the curry but the body of water also unfortunately.

3. **Morning Glory** - for fans of the Manchester band, Oasis, it has to be reference to one of their best-known albums "(What's the Story) Morning Glory". Also if you look for "morning glory" on the inter net there is reference to a British flower by that name but mostly it is sex stuff (educational at least for me) referring to

early hours sex and drugs. However I am much more at home with "morning glory" being the common name for South Asian water spinach. Although I do accept that "Oasis" did not write songs about exotic vegetables. The edible plant grows abundantly in waterways all over South East Asia and as such it is not unique to anywhere in particular. However one key holiday destination in the region, Thailand, likes to think of "morning glory" as being primarily an important member of their cuisine. There is powerful opposition to that suggestion from the most expansive neighbours India and China. The Chinese refer to our plant as "Chinese water spinach". Why is it big counties always want to takeover things whether it is more land or simply dishes shared with others? I like to think of "morning glory" as having a special home in Laos, there are many dishes requiring the plant, it is virtually a Laotian staple with huge numbers of locals regularly eating the plant mostly stir fried. A simple way of preparing the plant "morning glory" is to wok cook the chopped plant, leaves and hollow stem, in fresh chilli, garlic, soy sauce and oyster sauce and serve it up with meat or fish. "Morning glory" has that classic spinach taste while it is said the vegetable also has some pepperiness reminiscent of watercress and I think that to be the case.

4. **Broken Rice** - broken tech, broken ankle, broken glass, broken records, broken promises or even a broken heart but broken rice seems more than a bit extreme. On the other hand wherever in the World rice is grown and harvested, broken rice grains are an

inevitable consequence of all that milling and the like. In most places, broken rice is set aside and sometimes used as animal feed. Whereas in the West, broken rice mostly is used for industrial purposes to create starch. Traditionally in a number of countries broken rice is eaten by the poor who can't afford to buy anything better. Having said that in some places it is an important dish an example is Vietnam where broken rice is a key part of a celebrated dish and that is in Vietnam's Saigon (now called Ho Chi Minh City). In this town broken rice has re-invented itself from being despised food to becoming a must have item. It appears the broken rice is a key street food specialty called "com tam" where the rice is accompanied by pork steak (often barbequed), pork scratchings and a fried egg plus other garnishings. Salad items and pickles are common accompaniments and dipping sauce is an essential requirement. The broken rice grains release excessive starch when they are cooking so the end product should be reasonably sticky. As a test of stickiness the bowl of cooked broken rice is inverted on the plate and removed to leave behind a compact dome. "Com tam" is now becoming a key dish throughout the whole of Vietnam and, through tourism, it is being adopted elsewhere in the World. "Cracked rice', like whole "paella rice" and "risotto rice", is now more appreciated because of its ability to absorb flavour something the Vietnamese chefs know way back in the past. It does seem an irony that a waste product up until recent times now is often sold as an exotic foodstuff. If you don't believe me look at the price of a bag of broken rice in specialist shops or on line.

MALAYSIA AND SINGAPORE

1. **Bread John** - you could name your bread almost any name you like but John - a toilet? That seems totally bizarre at least to me. The name of the bread in Malaya is "roti John". Now Malaya to a slightly lesser extent, like its neighbour Singapore, has social and cuisine influences from very large countries quite close by. Malaya and Singapore have large and economically influential Chinese populations that have helped mold the character of both places. Equally influential are the countries' Pakistani, Bangladeshi and Indian settlers that have adopted these lands as their home. Of course a "roti" is an Indian flatbread so it did not originate in either Malaya or Singapore although in both places they are popular eating. The enthusiasm for "roti" in Malaya is widespread and not just limited to the ethnic Indian subcontinent population. However our specific "roti john" began life back in the 1960s not as a bready treat for locals but as a tourist indulgence. A holidaymaker asked a Malaysian street hawker for a "burger". At the time McDonalds and Burger King were still in their

infancy so what might a burger be? The hawker got the beef mince component and the bread right but the portion of mince was limited and the bread rather large. He had a brainwave and stuffed in a well-cooked omelet to bulk out the filling. This is Malaya so you need a dip or two with every dish but what goes with this strange egg and mince filled roti? What to do? Just go to extremes and provide mayonnaise for creaminess and hot sauce for fire and let the customer decide - brilliant! But then there is the ultimate question why call a "roti John"? Well the Brits were around in Malaya in large numbers in the 1960s and not entirely popular in some quarters since the grim fighting in the 1950s and Malayan independence in 1957. Quite a few of those Brits had strange unpronounceable names but "John" or "John something" that's easy. If they were not "Johns" who cares! As a result hawkers of those times referred to all white foreigners as "Johns" also they didn't even have to be those wretched Brits. As time passed the "roti for a John" evolved into "roti John" and in addition the Brits became OK tourists. To some of the older hawkers we are still "Johns" while "roti john" of course is to be had from stalls and carts throughout the country but now it is enjoyed by tourists and locals alike. A burger and egg in a flatbread is decent eating doused in hot sauce but forget the mayo in my opinion!

2. **Brains** - my grandfather loved offal in most of its forms. He enjoyed stewed or fried liver, kidneys were an essential component of any steak pie, sweetbreads made an appearance as a supper delicacy as did tripe on

Sunday evenings. However he drew the line at eating brains. "We are not cannibals from Pacific islands nor (even worse) those bloody French thank the Lord!" He was in a cavalry regiment during WWI and Granpa and his beloved horse survived the carnage. He came home to Scotland but his horse (as did most of the WWI horses) went to feed starving French and Belgian civilians. Whom it was rumored ate everything but the hooves - horse brains included. Now at least in the eating sense, most countries in Europe do not have the sensitivities of grandfather and the rest of the UK. Indeed France does have dishes like "cervelle de veau" (calf brains) but round the World, brain eating tends to relate more to necessity rather than exotic luxury. Our Singaporean and Malayan "brains" is called "otak otak" in Malay however they are nothing to do with actual brains but looks a bit like brains. It is a combination of macerated fish (such as mackerel, snapper, grouper, wrasse and others) with a complex spice paste (that includes chilli, galangal, garlic, lemongrass, turmeric, ginger and many others) all bound together with some coconut milk. The reddish mixture is locked within two bits of banana leaf then stitched closed with sharp toothpicks. The dish can be steamed, oven cooked or heated up in a dry wok. In addition I have had "otak otak" in Singapore cooked on the barbeque so giving the fish paste mix a rather smoky taste. I was brought up on sandwiches of fish paste from a jar, this is a more exotic version of the same but still doesn't merit lining up for seconds!

3. **Burnt Fish** - no matter where you live in the World some people like their food more than just well cooked but burning your food is another level surely? That nasty smell in the kitchen and you know you should have checked earlier and now your meal is fit only for the bin. Mostly true but there are exceptions for instance the well-loved French dessert "crème brulee" is actually a Scots creation called "burnt cream". In Mediterranean cooking, "roasted peppers" are burnt on the flames to bring a charred dimension to the flavour and much the same is done with "USA barbeque brisket" that looks terrible on the outside from the smoker but wonderful within. Burning corn in Mexico brings extra sweetness to the kernels while burnt rice at the base of a paella pan in Spain is a treat as is "bottom of the pot" in Iran (see earlier). Mind you despite all these exceptions to the burning rule, Malaysian "burnt fish" seems a step too far? You find the dish all over Malaysia (and Indonesia for that matter) but particularly in the big cities like Kuala Lumpur. Whole fish, like mackerel, grouper or red snapper, are cooked on a grill where they get some protection from the fierce heat by a layer of banana leaves on the bars. Delicate fillets of white fish, skate or ray wings and even seafood like squid need even more layers of leaves. The fish for the dish they call locally "Ikan (fish) bakar (burnt)", gets a thick coating of "sambal" which is a marinade rich in chilli, shrimp paste and onion. The fierce, short cooking at high temperature blackens the banana leaves, the marinade and the fish. Not the prettiest supper to admire but no matter the look of the outside charring, inside the fish

is moist and tasty as only quick cooking can achieve. Some chemical magic takes place such that the fire smoke, the charcoaled banana leaves and the blacked marinade all contribute an earthiness combined with a nutty complexity and a spice-laden richness to the juicy "ikan bakar". Usually the dish is completed with a small bowl of rice and a dipping sauce. It doesn't need much else and the smoky smell is extraordinary.

4. **Carrot Cake** - I make the very best "carrot cake" in the whole Universe and that is based on expert opinion. Well at least I get feedback from family members and they are all very opinionated! I do eat the carrot cake made by others - just so I can give them friendly advice on where they are doing wrong if you know what I mean? Set them back on the proper path and all that. The truth is I can't pass a cake shop or café by that has carrot cake in the window. It is an addiction but a very tasty one. Then one fateful day in the mid 1980s I was in Singapore and told by some local fiend who advised me, the carrot cake addict, that "chai tow kway" was their must have "carrot cake". Of course I wrote the name in my "filofax" (no don't laugh they were the essential yuppie business planner from those times) and set my mind to having a Singaporean carrot cake as soon as possible. It turns out Singaporeans, despite massive British influence from the early 19th Century onwards, had no idea what might constitute a decent "carrot cake". Way back in the mid 1980s, this was a place where my kids could eat "angle delight" or pots of "Chivers jellies" almost everywhere on Santosa Island.

In addition my son Stewart was able to finish off three bowls of "Brown Windsor soup" during Sunday Lunch at the old Raffles Hotel. Even today there are plenty of English theme restaurants where you can get everything from "fish and chips" to "steak and kidney pie"! So "carrot cake" had to be easy peasy! Then we heard a local place did "carrot cake" for breakfast - seems a strange breakfast item but still? Turned out nice sweet cake it wasn't - it consisted of chopped daikon (radish), rice flour, eggs, garlic, spring onions, soy sauce and chilli sauce. All this was fried off in a wok and served in a bowl. I looked down at this strange fry up and said forlornly "we ordered carrot cake". Our friendly water said "this is "chai tow kway" our "carrot cake" but plenty vegetables though no carrots!" A carrot-less, non-cake savoury stir fry called "carrot cake" - at this point we all felt far, far from home.

INDONESIA

1. **Devil's Soup** - the dish originates in Surabaya in Java and is a key member of the "rawon" family of meat soups or thin stews. Javanese like their meat and dishes such as "Java roast beef" are well known throughout the islands so it's not surprising they are also keen on meaty soups and stews. Java is by no means the biggest of the Indonesian islands but it is by far the most populous being home to 145 million Indonesians. It is the economic hub and the capital Jakarta is a cosmopolitan city with history going way back to the colonial times of the Dutch East Indies. Java is a cigar shaped island with Jakarta to the west looking out towards Sumatra. The city of Surabaya is towards the eastern end of Java and we are at the home of "rawon setan" the so-called "Devil's Soup". I've not been to Surabaya but I have been to the island of Bali, a stone's throw away where "rawon" also is enjoyed. The "devil's soup" consists of beef chunks in a rich beef stock full of spices including galangal, lemongrass, garlic, spring onions, kaffir lime leaves, candlenut, ginger, turmeric and others. As you can tell it is a rich mix but the dominant component of the stock is "keluak nut" by no means exclusive to

Indonesia. However "keluak" has a dark reputation, the plant is poisonous needing careful processing to become edible. Once processed, the nut gives dishes a distinct flavour but also an intense black colour (like squid ink). Now-a-days the meaty soup is available in restaurants from breakfast onwards; at one time it was a late night treat only! Late night eating when mischief is traditionally afoot, the intense black colour of the stock and the poison in the "keluak plant" all conspire to make it the "soup of the devil".

2. **Submarine** - the very first submarine from the was made by a Dutchman Cornelius Drebbel out of a rowing boat and covered with some greased hides. Back in the 17th Century the submarine craft navigated 15 feet under the Thames - brave sailors indeed! About 100 years later during the American War of Independence the Americans developed an attack submarine called the Turtle. Move on 200 years and you have the nuclear submarine that is the most frightening sea vessel either above or below the waves. Submarines have acquired a quite distinctive shape such that various cuisines describe food as being submarine-like but the best known has to be the American "submarine sandwich". An elongated soft roll packed with all sorts of fillings hot and cold. It is said that the Italian immigrant who came up with the idea for this range of sandwiches did so after seeing a submarine in a US museum. On the other hand our Indonesian submarine is a different beast altogether that lurks primarily on the Island of Sumatera but now is spread throughout South East Asia. "Pempek" are

a wide group of foods rather like fishcakes and one of these "pempek kapal selam" is the "submarine". Essentially a fish dough is created out of macerated fish, seasoning, egg, tapioca starch, (some times additional flour) and water. The pempek dough is wrapped around a raw egg, sealed and boiled so it is cooked through. Thereafter the "pempek kapal selam" is deep fried, served up with a cucumber salad, perhaps noodles and always a sugar, vinegar, tamarind, garlic and cayenne pepper dip referred to as "cuko". Thus the Sumatran submarine is created and the mariner inside is a double cooked egg! Now the eggy "pembek kapal selam) are as often diving bell shaped as submarine like (at least to me). However when in boiling water the "pempek" falls to the bottom (submerges) but when cooked it surfaces (a very submarine-like action perhaps?).

3. **Spicy-spicy** - it stands to reason that spicy-spicy from North Sulawesi has really got a serious kick to it! Sulawesi is a strange looking island; a small body with four huge arms. The very longest arm is to the north and towards its end is the city of Manado. It is here that "spicy-spicy" came into existence under its local name of "rica-rica". Our "spicy-spicy" is not a dish as such but the spice paste mix, central to the creation of many rich but tasty dishes. The base of the sauce is plenty of chilli and in addition there is chopped onion, garlic, ginger, lemongrass and kaffir lime leaves. "Rica-rica" type dishes can be meat, seafood or tasty vegetarian options but the best known is the chicken dish known widely as "ayam rica-rica". Essentially you take chicken,

lemon, tomato and a few additional spices, cook them all together enriched by your "rica-rica" preparation. You end up with a special dish that has a little tomato, loads of fiery chilli and in addition a bit of a sour citrus note. Sad type people who get too involved with food (oh dear) might have a few tingles and think - "where have I heard of foods like this elsewhere?" Well in Goa there is there is that vinegar and really hot curry rich in chilli we call "vindaloo" (see India earlier) and in Mozambique there is "piri piri" so loved in southern Africa and throughout the World for its sour heat. Of course it is those Portuguese explorers who took their enthusiasm for vinegar soaked meat and South American tomatoes but particularly chilli to all corners of the World. One of these corners was the island of Celebes, which today is known as Sulawesi in Indonesia.

PHILIPPENES

1. **Soup Number 5** - the Philippines is an archipelago of islands; in this case one hell of a lot of islands given that there are well over 7,500 of them it seems. I wonder who had the computer and did all the counting? Way back when the Spanish were top dogs in terms of sailing the World's oceans they got hold of the archipelago and had it named after their King Phillip - Las Philipinas. The religious and social legacy is that the country was then, and still remains, predominantly Catholic Christian (over 80%). The Philippines came under American control for a while and finally became independent in 1946 after WWII. Unlike some of their close neighbours who are governed by the dietary rules of Islam, the Philippines for the most part really enjoy pork and beef as well as a wide range of fish and meats ranging from chicken to goat. Pork is very prominent and, in common with many parts of South East Asia, suckling pig ("lechon") is the "must have" festival dish. However locals like to eat up everything so dishes like "sisig" (ears and bits of pig head) are household treats. Clearly if Filipinos are careful with pig then it is also the case with the more expensive beef - literally everything is eaten up.

It is taken to an absolute extreme in the case of "soup number 5" which is a spicy broth containing chopped up ox penis and testicles as the meat content. Surely you would need to be desperate to eat this concoction? No, it is much admired by male Filipinos who think it is an aphrodisiac. Further it seems to be the case that the more adventurous type of tourist likes to take on "soup No.5" as a more than exotic challenge. Why is it called "soup No.5"? Well it is often placed in the 5th position on the soup menu in the street side food stalls or indoor cafés. A more bloke-type explanation is that the soup contains the 5th member of the bull - lets leave it at that please I'm quivering a little!

2. **Beer Chow** - in the Philippines the adults on a night out do like to have something nice to eat when they have a drink. The Filipinos are not alone in this. The Spanish have to have their "tapas" while the Italians as they sup enjoy a wide range of "apertivo." For that matter most countries offer food in their bars and cafes these days. Even those few countries were the bars were traditionally drinks only like Britain, Ireland, Australia and the USA have gone some way in recent years to catch up with everyone else. Pubs in my Dad's day served crisps and pork scratchings if you were lucky. By my time the selection had increased to pickled eggs and a few lunchtime cheese and ham rolls. While these days my grown up children select a pub often for the bar snacks and three course meals they offer rather than just the booze. Our Filipino drinkers do like their ice-cold beer but they like their "pulutan"

also which in English (the second language there) is of course "beer chow". The chow is as wide ranging as Spanish tapas but Filipinos do have great enthusiasm for pork when they are in the bar (or out of it). Freshly made "pork scratchings' ("chicharon"), crispy "pork belly" on a stick (their "lechon kawali") and barbeque pork of various types are popular examples. Other "beer chow" favourites include raw "tuna slices" (or other fish) in vinegar with onions, chillis and ginger ("kinilaw"), "dried anchovies" fried crisp (known locally as "dilis") and Filipino-style "Chinese beef" (called "chowking"). If you visit these islands, grab some Filipino "chow" with your cold beer and enjoy!

3. **Berigg** - please don't look up the recipe for "berigg" because I made the name up! Even if it were a real word, it doesn't sound too much like an exotic Philippine dish far more like the name of a remote UK village. I have just created rather pathetically what is a possible portmanteau word that Anglicizes what is a real portmanteau word in Philippine cuisine called "tapsilog". I have to say I would rather ask for a "tapsilog" than my "berigg" and that is a key feature of any portmanteau word; it needs to slip off the tongue easily. Thanks for sticking with me on this I do tend to ramble at times! Words that are created by sticking a bit of one word with another (or even more) are called portmanteaus after the old fashioned carry cases. We don't tend to have portmanteau cases these days but back in Victorian times they were a combination of two identical sections to make the one suitcase. In language they are segments of at least two

words making one word that means the same as the two separately. There are masses of computer examples such as email (electronic mail), malware (malicious software) or political ones that include Brexit (Britain exit) and for us Scots Inderef (Independence Referendum) or even some foodie ones such as spam (spiced ham), silk (soy mixed with milk), also grastropub (gastronomy public house) and so it goes on. Back to the Philippines our "tapsilog" is a portmanteau that stretches to 3 elements that make the final word. "Tapa" is thin sliced, salted or marinated, beef while "sinangag" is a nutritious but compact portion of refried rice with plenty of sliced garlic and the third element itlog is a classic sunny side up fried egg. Combine the word parts and you have a Philippine breakfast enjoyed by many locals especially if it has a sharp dipping sauce sauce. If you then pair the dish with pickle and a salad you have a classic backpacker brunch (breakfast and lunch). So my English portmanteau version of "tapsilog" is much the same consisting of beef, rice and egg so making my "berigg". I'll stop playing about now and state quite categorically that a fried egg paired with tasty and garlic-rich quality rice plus thin spicy beef makes a perfect meal any time of the day or night. Whether taken for breakfast or supper, do remember you always need a sharp, vinegar-rich dipping sauce; it is an Indonesian specialty after all.

4. **Adidas** - now we are getting silly surely? In the beginning the mighty "Adidas" company was a small affair started by Adi Dassler (another portmanteau word - see earlier) in the early years of the 20th Century. The company

set out to make sports equipment for German athletes competing in a wide range of events. Their breakthrough came in 1954 when the German football team won the World cup wearing "Adidas" boots. The company went from strength to strength and launched its iconic trefoil logo at the Munich Olympics of 1972. From then on it diversified and expanded to become the worldwide brand it is today. Global "Adidas" may be, but what is the link with street traders in the Philippines? Well it is nothing to do with tracksuits, football boots or even trainers although masses of these "Adidas" products are sold in the shops and markets in those Islands. It is however a lot to do with feet but in this case it is "chicken's feet"! The "chicken feet" dish is a mid 20th Century creation and for older Filipinos a "waste nothing" meal from times of poverty. As years past "Adidas" has become a special treat and for some the preferred part of the fowl. On Mainland China crunching chickens' feet goes back centuries although they were never considered frugal food as in the Philippines but a treat for Emperors. Our Filipino "chicken feet" or "adobong Adidas" are wok or pan cooked in lots of garlic, chilli, soy sauce and vinegar. The liquids boil down and thicken with gelatin from the cooked feet making a sticky, tasty coating then they are served often as "beer chow" (see previously) by street vendors. The dish is also served up in cafes where it is accompanied by rice and vegetables turning a street snack into a substantial meal. Why on earth do street vendors call their "chicken feet" snack "Adidas"? It is their joke - chickens have three toes and the Adidas logo is a trefoil.

CHINA

1. **Thousand Year Eggs** - sometimes they are described diminutively as one hundred year or century eggs. All these titles are exaggerations both in terms of time needed to prepare and how long the eggs remain edible (edible is a term I use very loosely). The dish for the most part uses duck eggs but goose or chicken eggs also will serve reasonably well. Essentially the eggs are preserved in their shells in a heady mixture of brine lime, ash and clay. Thereafter they are traditionally wrapped in mud and rice (or other cereal) husks for some weeks, even months, but certainly not years. The pH goes alkaline in the raw egg and as a result undergoes numerous chemical reactions. The curing process has the effect of solidifying the egg but with an entirely different end result compared to cooking whether that is frying, poaching or boiling. The albumin does not go white but turns into an amber/brownish jelly. While the yellow yolk doesn't solidify as such but gradually turns into a green paste. I have been offered "thousand year eggs" many times but eaten one processed duck egg only once. When peeled, the brown jelly has a dark sheen but slice the egg up and have a whiff of those escaping

gasses (ammonia, hydrogen sulphide and the like); they clear your sinuses ok but I was reduced to tears. The white, sorry yellow brown, has poor texture but the taste is tolerable although bland with a nasty lingering chemical after taste. If you are bold enough you taste the green paste. To me there is no hyper mature cheese I've ever eaten that quite compares (I have spent lots of time in France eating over ripe brie). After finishing the green stuff you quiver, not with anticipation but with considerable fear, you know your host will insist you "enjoy" the other half of your egg!

2. **Lion's Heads** - I lived near Liverpool for many years and enjoyed the China Town new years festivities on many occasions. They always were lively and exciting especially when the lion with its huge head made an appearance and danced for us all. Without doubt the lion is a potent symbol in Chinese society, a visual representation of massive power and authority. As a result huge lion statues guard all Chinese buildings of special importance such as palaces and the like. There are two extraordinary lions in the Forbidden City for example - one male and the other female. The male represents conquest while the female is the symbol of fertility. Modern China is still annexing land as if it did not have sufficient already and one in four of the World population is Chinese - wow grab me a lion statue it seems to work! Our Chinese dish of "lion's heads" ("shi zi tou") is made up of extremely large and rather fatty meatballs. Their main constituents are pork mince, egg, breadcrumbs and crushed chestnuts with

lots of soy sauce (in some parts of China a little vinegar is introduced also) to soften and moisten the mix. There are multiple ways of cooking the "lions heads" such as braising or alternatively cooking in a mild broth. The meatballs are usually served on a bed of steamed greens (Chinese cabbage) in preference to rice. It is argued that the cooked meatball on the serving plate looks like the back of a lion's head while the cabbage is a kind of mane. Ok, a very strange lion but perhaps that's just me. I'm a meatball man, people think my meatballs as superb - well only my daughter as it happens. I make my meatballs small, Swedish style, so can't get my head around these huge Chinese monsters but they taste great especially on a bed of lightly cooked green cabbage.

3. **Dragon in the Flame of Desire** - this dish on a menu sounds really impressive and what a dramatic meal it must be? A Chinese, dragon dish no less; that has to be something special surely? The dragon is everywhere in China, terracotta ones on roofs, symbolic versions on paintings, dragon statues everywhere from palaces to restaurants. You get a whole range of porcelain, plastic or paper dragons in ordinary homes. By way of contrast go back in time to when China was ruled by powerful Chinese emperors, then having replica dragons or motifs was forbidden because the royalty considered themselves descendants of ancient dragons so obviously they had all "dibs" on the beasts. In the West our dragons are malignant fire emitting creatures to be avoided at all cost whereas in the East they are considered to be water creatures that bring the vital rains to water the crops.

Above all else they are bringers of good fortune hence their presence everywhere in China. Dragons are drawn as being snake-like with big heads and legs so when it becomes "dragon in the flame of desire" we have a Chinese euphemism for the male organ - nasty! The dish is a roast yack's penis, rather a large roast I am told. Unlike "soup No 5" from the Philippines (see earlier), this is a specialist meal requested only by gourmets comfortable with Chinese fine dining. Regional Chinese food is wonderful but the formal banquets, replete with delicacies, can be a little taxing to the untrained pallet and the delicate tummy. I have not had the pleasure of tasting the poor old yack's private parts but truly there are "delights" I have sampled in China and Hong Kong that I would gladly have swapped for a chew on the yak's "dragon."

4. **Ants Climbing a Tree** - lots of ant species forage or even live their lives in trees. For example, weaver ants bind leaves together with silk strands to make their nests while carpenter ants burrow into wood. Leaf cutter ants slice up the canopy and take their leaf booty off to feed their fungus gardens underground. Ants can farm tree-damaging aphids for their honeydew while other ant species merely kill them. In turn ants can be dinner for all manner of animals including wolf spiders, lizards, right up to anteaters and pangolins. Surely not food for us? Well not strictly true many species are edible but have a sour taste it seems due to their formic acid. In Mexico dried or even chocolate-coated ants are bar snacks while in various parts of the World they are

served up coated with chilli powder. Personally I think I will stick to crisps and pork scratchings as my bar treat. None-the-less "ants climbing a tree" creates images that do not give most of us much of an appetite. As it turns out our "ants climbing a tree" are not real ants at all. If you can just get past the name then the reward is the enjoyment of a truly delicious dish. In Chinese it is "Ma Yi Shang Shu" and it consists of thin translucent cellophane noodles, best quality pork mince, crushed garlic, sliced red chilli and chopped spring onions in a rich red bean paste, soy and oyster sauce. It is a classic member of the cuisine of the culinary significant Sichuan Province. Sichuan is a colder area of China and so they like a little warm spiciness in their food. When the dish is all put together the mince sticks to the savoury noodles in a way that reminds the Chinese of all those many "ants climbing a tree".

TAIWAN

1. **Stinky Tofu** - without doubt tofu has become a more popular food in Britain these days. Essentially it is processed "soya bean" that is soaked, crushed, boiled and separated. If you think of milk being turned into curds (solids) and whey (liquid) then the tofu procedure first produces pulp and a bean milk. The milk is acidified and from that comes a kind of whey that is removed and a solid that becomes the basic tofu. Depending on the processing, the resultant tofu is extra soft, silken, firm or extra firm. Tofu production has been around in China for 2 thousand years or more and from there it came to Japan and South East Asian countries. Tofu is the Japanese name for the product whereas in China (Mandarin) it is "doufu". Outside it's home countries, it has been a rather despised foodstuff for centuries but in recent times it has become trendy. After all it is rich in minerals, low in calories and there is a total absence of cholesterol also it is solidly vegan and healthy. "Tofu" for the most part is pretty tasteless but its saving grace is it absorbs flavour before and during cooking. "Tofu" flavourings, if required, are as varied as your tastes and range from soy sauce and vinegar to lemon

and sugar syrup. The "stinky tofu" is a different beast altogether and very much a Taiwanese specialty though it undoubtedly comes from mainland China and is also eaten in Hong Kong and Vietnam. During processing the "tofu" is exposed to a salt solution infused with vegetable and fish matter. Essentially these additionals can vary but bamboo, greens of various sorts, a few herbs and lots of dried fish and prawns are central to the mix. The "tofu" is then left in its fermenting brine for months to take on "character". In Taiwan they like to fry "stinky tofu" and serve it in bite sized blocks with pickled cabbage, chilli sauce and a range of other toppings. Do a lot of restaurants serve it? Virtually no restaurant serves "stinky tofu" if they want to stay in business. It stinks like an old tramp's armpit and the smell is even worse when frying the stuff. No, "stinky tofu" is the preserve of street traders and night market stalls. Very much an outdoors "enjoyment" for the aficionados of "tofu" gone more than a bit high. Indeed in the travel brochures and Taiwanese food guides "stinky tofu" is described as smelling like a ripe "stilton" or perhaps "camembert". That is extreme wishful thinking; some of us would smear runny "camembert" on their nostrils to relieve themselves of the pong of "stinky tofu". One well-known TV chef compared "stinky tofu" unfavourably with the contents of a baby's nappy - it does have that raw sewerage reek about it. I am prepared to accept that "stinky tofu" has its admirers and a gourmet following who say despite the smell it tastes wonderful. My thoughts on the matter are to try one piece but have a hanky close by when you spit it out.

2. **Coffin Buns** Taiwan was occupied by the Japanese during WWII and at war end in 1945 the country's economy and food production was in a mess. Much of this was due to continuous allied bombing during the later war years. Rice production was down dramatically so the USA provided masses of cereal but this was mostly wheat not rice. Taiwan needed lots of help to get back on its feet through the post war years especially when its population was boosted by over 2 million refugees escaping the communist take over of Mainland China. Going from a rice-based diet to a rice and wheat one had implications that influence Taiwanese cuisine to this day. The people still like their rice but they eat plenty of noodles (rice or wheat) and enjoy their breads (wheat). Soft milk bread loaf is admired far and wide and spring onion flatbreads are loved in Taiwan as they are in China. Pepper buns for instance have a peppery pork mince filling covered by a bread/pastry-like crispy shell and cooked in a tandoor. Taiwanese "coffin bread" turns out to be unusual both in name and composition. It came into existence in the markets of the old City of Tainan back in those difficult years of the 1940s. Although you can get "coffin bread" throughout Taiwan, to this day it is still associated with Tainan particularly its food stalls, markets and restaurants. A big block of white bread is hollowed out and the lid kept then both are deep-fried. This is not so much the meal itself but more the edible container for your supper. The hollow in the fried bread is filled with a thick shellfish, chicken or vegetarian stew and the lid popped back on. South Africans eat "bunny chow", an empty round loaf topped up with curry. In

Britain and the USA a specialty dish is a round crusty farmhouse loaf hollowed out and filled with a hearty beef and vegetable stew. The Americans often go a step further and fill their hollowed bread with "chowder". I think there is a strong probability the Tainan vendors got their idea for "coffin bread" from American chowder in a loaf. The give away is that the "coffin" contents are frequently topped with grated cheese a favourite USA topping for their "chowders".

3. **Chicken Bums** - no it isn't a spelling issue, it is not "chicken buns" it is "bums" (as in Britain) or more often "butts" (as in America). Now it is a long time since I got my Zoology degree but I know a "chicken ass" is not an "ass" as we know it from our own human anatomy. Yes it is absolutely obvious the "chicken bum" is nice and fluffy whereas we don't (unless rather kinky) have feathers sticking out of our butts. Less obvious is that the chicken, as is the case for all birds, does not have an anus. An anus, being the opening at the end of our digestive tract, is where we get rid of undigested food waste, fibre, bacteria from the digestive tract, water and other indigestibles. To us, it is just excrement and an anus has only one job getting shot of it. The chicken has a cloaca that does three jobs in the female. It passes eggs, this opening takes in sperm from the male to fertilize eggs and when appropriate releases waste from the digestive system. In may be obvious but hens (as with all birds) don't pee, instead uric acid coats their faeces and of course burns the paint off your car. In Taiwan "chicken butts" on a stick are choice eating.

Imagine some people prefer "bums" to other choice cuts of chicken while paying good money for their delicacy. As far as I know the "butt" eaters do not have ageusia (the medical word for no sense of taste) nor are they inmates of mental institutions as far as I know. But "chicken butts" abound in night markets and there is a roaring trade in this delicacy. The "bums" are first boiled, then well spiced and seasoned before being deep-fried until crispy. Now with some soy sauce they are ready for eating. This is one of the few times in this book that the dishes name describes what you get except of course you are eating cloaca not anus - what a bummer!

4. **Frog's Egg Tea** - now there is "black tea", "green tea", even "white tea" and a whole range of spice or herb infusion teas but "frog's egg tea" now that's a really strange one don't you think? Come Spring and out come the flowers, the trees are in bud, birds are busy nesting, bees are buzzing and if you have a garden pond the shallows should be packed with little spheres of jelly with black dots in the middle - thousands of them! Frogs eggs abound, they have to because as they develop in the jelly and when they are free swimming tadpoles they are fair game to every thing including birds, fish, hedgehogs and even carnivorous dragonfly larvae. If 10% of the eggs become tadpoles then that is a good result and on top of that few tadpoles will make it to become fully grown frogs! You can add humans to the list of frog predators for example the French still like their frog leg starters. However it is South East Asia

where frog farms abound and the clients are not averse to eating frogspawn in addition to the adults. In Taiwan there is an enthusiasm for eating snake so frogs and frogspawn are child's play. As it turns out however our drink of choice is not based on actual frogspawn but on tapioca! Funny enough tapioca pudding at school dinners was always called frogspawn back in the day. Numerous countries understand the frogspawn-tapioca thing and Taiwan is one of those but in addition they have a strange liking for tapioca. These days "frog egg tea" is often called "bubble tea" making it sound a little more commercial. It seems to have come into being in Taiwan teahouses back in the 1980s when a scoop or two of sweet tapioca was combined with tea. The "bubbles" or "frog's eggs" are little "tapioca pearls" so to make the tea or "boba" at home take hot tea, tapioca pearls, milk and lots of sugar serve warm or cold. The tapioca needs to be boiled for a while before use but "frog's eggs tea" is simple to make. These days the tea is usually served in a glass with a wide milkshake straw and the tea can be all sorts of flavours and colours.

KOREAN PENINSULA

1. **Hangover Stew** - I think every culture that enjoys a good drink every now and then has a hangover cure to fall back on - perhaps just to fall over on! In my home country of Scotland we swear by a greasy fry up in a bun and a fizzy drink called "Irn Bru". A sugar hit and a fat-rich nightmare for the arteries but very tasty. Russians know all about hangovers but their cure is just a nightmare - the vinegar juice from a pickle jar. The Canadians soak up the excess booze with "poutine" a pile of chips, gravy and curd cheese. Aussies are into egg and avocado on toast when they are "under the weather" (I highly recommend this tasty dish sober or drunk). I'm not so sure of some other nations' options however. From samurai times the Japanese hangover cure is salty, extremely sour plums - hari kari is marginally more unpleasant. Oh sorry, perhaps worse than salty sour plums or painful suicide is the Mongolian cure - a "bloody Mary" that includes sheep's eyes. Now there are various hangover stews - rice porridge from Thailand, eggs in hot milk is the Columbian solution, Ugandans help you sober up with a stew of mashed banana and goat offal and there is another involving tripe (Puerto

Rico). Our South Korean "hangover stew" is called "haejangguk" locally. It is a spicy, often fiery beef stew or soup (cubed beef or ox bones more traditionally) with local cabbage, radish, spring onions, dried mushrooms and bean sprouts. It is made in all sorts of ways but delicious with "kimchi" on the side. By the way if you must have a hangover best it be in Korea rather than Mongolia (just a thought).

2. **Rice Thief** - is a Korean dish of several names but a common one is "ganjang gejang" that I believe translates to soy sauce crab (sauce) or some such. It is best known locally as the "rice thief". Now this is not a nice pile of crabmeat with a little soy sauce on the side; no our preparation is far more exotic than that. For our delicacy, and in Korea it is quite a sought after delicacy, live crabs (or frozen live crabs) are submerged in a type of special extra salty soy sauce and pickled! "Rice thief" is not something new in Korea, it was a dish served up to princes back in the 17th Century. At that time it seems soy was not the specific "embalming fluid" for the crabs but a cocktail of salt, rice wine and other alcohol did the job instead. Then until recent times the female Chinese mitten crab, replete with abundant roe, was preferred above all other crab options for the dish. Unfortunately the mitten crab lives in rivers and estuaries that have become badly polluted. It is a tough character and survives ok but this crustacean is no longer suitable for a dish that involves uncooked meat. Horse crabs among others are the current favourites. They are frozen and then submerged in the soy sauce brine plus a little

chilli, lemon, ginger and garlic. The pickling takes up to three days with two changes of soy or more. Break up your crab and serve it up with the roe, some salty marinade, chillis, sliced cucumber and spring onion on rice. The meal is rich so you will go through a lot of rice to counteract the luxurious, heady crab flavours that make it "the thief of rice".

3. **Fake Meat** - I understand "injobap" translates into English as "fake meat" and when I first heard of it, I thought it must be North Korea's version of USA "spam". However when they say fake they mean vegetarian fake and the meal is cheaper than chips. North Korea is a force to be reckoned with in military terms even down to having a nuclear weapons arsenal, long-range missiles and an army in excess of 1 million. Incredible for such a small nation but economically there is a price to pay and the average citizen is extremely poor. Indeed it got so bad in the 1990s that famine resulted in the death of millions. Relatively things have got better for the population but North Koreans still find it hard to make ends meet. Our dish comes from the hardest of times and was created during the famine years. I am told "injobap" is fully vegan and tastes really good. Sadly no one I know has the complete recipe for the "fake meat" part but it involves leftover tofu, bean curd and spices. Thereafter the non-meat creation is spread around a lump of sticky rice and smothered with a sweet sauce. It is one of my ambitions to try fake meat and have the complete recipe - how sad is that!

4. **Sundae** - is an indulgent ice cream in a really tall glass, lots of scoops, fruit, sprinkles and sauces. The "sundae" originated in America and went forth from their ice cream parlors around the World. It Britain they transformed into the infamous "knickerbocker glory" that inhabited seaside resorts. In the 1960s my Aunt Jen spent much of each year as the grumpy slimming lady. Then off she would go Blackpool or some other place and pig out on "knickerbocker glories". She would come home the happy smiling fat lady we all adored. I do not think Jen would be happy or smiling if she had a Korean sundae because that is "a horse of a different color" as the Wizard of Oz and Shakespeare might say. As well as "sundae" it is also represented in English as "soondae" and turns out to be a rather exotic black pudding sausage enjoyed in both North and South Korea. The sausage has an incredibly long history going back perhaps as far as the 10th Century. In addition the pig's blood of the sausage seems to have been mixed with almost anything that came to hand. Cereal, noodles, onion, soybean, bean sprouts and even in some regions seafood gets into the blood sausage mix. "Sundae" is a meal in its own right and sold as street food but it is also used to bulk out all manner of dishes from soups to dry dishes.

JAPAN

1. **Cherry Blossom Meat** (sakura niku or basashi) - it is thin slices of horsemeat flavoured with ginger, other spices and soy sauce. It is part of sushi and sushimi tradition eaten uncooked with or without rice. There is a cultural taboo about horse eating in numerous English speaking countries, also eating raw meat is rather underwhelming to many individuals in Britain. On the other hand the French and many others in Continental Europe have no such compunctions (see also "brains" under Malaysia and Singapore earlier). After all the horse taboo is rather contradictory given that we Brits eat plenty other animals that can run, fly or swim. Historically it is worth remembering that horses became domesticated on the Russian Steps over 5,000 years ago but were good eating well before that. Basically the early horsemen from Central Asia were galloping about on their supper! Indeed the invading Tartars and Mongols of the 13th Century never rode anywhere without a mix of horsemeat and herbs in their back pockets. Heavy riding tenderized the raw meat ready for a cold dinner. Europeans liked the idea but substituted beef for horse so the highly prized "steak tartare" of today originated

under an ancient horseman's backside. I believe that makes "cherry blossom meat" seem rather ordinary - but still not the first meal I would choose in Japan.

2. **Sliced and Broiled** - sounds to me a bit like a medieval execution however I believe that to be the translation of "sukiyaki" a dish with a fine reputation in Japanese cuisine as a special dinner. It came to that country with the Chinese in the middle of the 19th Century. "Sukiyaki" is a light beef stew where often the thin slices of meat ("suki") are grilled ("yaki") and then added to a black pot containing a saucy broth plus noodles, tofu and a range of vegetables. The pot in placed in the middle of the table and everyone helps in the cooking and serving experience. Communal preparation and interactive eating is the key to the meal with boiled rice, a mix of pickles and plenty raw egg on the side. My Japanese friends and past colleagues told me "sukiyaki" is rarely eaten in modern Japan but when it is the event is always a treat. Unlike its cousin "teriyaki" now a supermarket special that is available everywhere. "Teriyaki" can be prepared in many ways but in its original form the meat was marinated before cooking, the sauce had foreign constituents like garlic and even pineapple. A key feature of the dish is that it is hugely versatile. Actually "teriyaki" was created in Hawaii (by immigrant Japanese cooks) and remains more American than Japanese to this day. Indeed on the mainland, Seattle also has a claim for being the original home of "teriyaki". Not that the famous "sukiyaki" has historic Japanese credentials as we know but it isn't

Chinese either. No the "slice and broil" meat followed by boiling in a pot with vegetables etc was a Mongolian dish and cooking procedure. The elegant Japanese black pot originally was a Mongolian soldier's helmet used for broiling over a cooking fire.

3. **Steamed Teacup** - I understand that the Japanese "chawanmushi" translates to "chawan" being a teacup and "mushi" steamed. Yes the Japanese do have this very elaborate tea ceremony involving spiritualism and Zen Buddhist principles. The participants become involved in a ritual during which they seek inner peace. The whole ceremony can take a few hours to complete, which is a long time to be kneeling on cushions! The ceremony does involve teacups and green tea but no steaming goes on that I know of. Our "steamed teacup" is not a drink but a meal involving a specialized teacup with a lid called a "chawanmushi" cup that often is rather beautiful and ornate in that Japanese style whereby small ordinary things are equally worthy of care and attention. Actually they are more like large egg coddlers than teacups but that's just my opinion. Somewhere in our kitchen there are a number of porcelain egg coddlers with metal lids. You butter the insides of each coddler, crack in eggs, pour over some cream and scatter on spring onions and close the lids. The eggs are then cooked in the oven in a water bath (bain marie). An old fashioned but rather nice way of eating eggs rarely done these days. Our "chawanmushi" is the Japanese equivalent of our once popular egg coddling only a bit more exotic and still very much in vogue. The chef makes an egg

custard made from eggs, stock, soy sauce and mirin (rice wine). It is then folded gently together and placed in the "chawanmushi" cup. A few treats go on top such as peeled cooked prawn, shiitaki mushrooms, chopped spring onion, ginko nut and sliced fish cake. The cup is steam cooked until the egg custard sets, then it is ready to enjoy!

4. **Sumo Stew** - my Japanese friends for the most part are short, slim and elegant. It reminds me that the Japanese diet is for the most part really good involving fresh vegetables lightly cooked, fish and not much in the way of red meat. There are exceptions however and one group who have no such balance to their diet are athletes who, in their home land, are treated like superstars. Sumo wrestling, at the professional level, is a male only business that has been around for many hundreds of years and is steeped in tradition and the teachings of the ancient Shinto religion. The combat takes place in a dojo ring and the object is straight forward and that simply is to push or manipulate your opponent out of the ring. There are no weight divisions in Sumo, so as size matters in this business, the pressure for success involves increasing the pounds by hearty eating. Training is intense so they may well be big (400 to 600lbs) but they are also immensely strong. They get to their optimum weight by gorging hefty meals but it remains more or less the same meal every time called "chanko nabe". The nickname for the dish is "Sumo stew" - it is made up of all sorts of healthy stuff including vegetables, tofu, fish and meat with rice on

the side and helpings of noodles to go into the broth when all the rest of the solid things have been polished off. A Sumo wrestler does not bother with breakfast; instead he works really hard until lunchtime and has his "chanko nabe". There after, at the end of the day, our wrestler has the same dinner again. Now a well-fed normal male might take in around 2,500 calories/day but by comparison two full athlete-sized "chanko nabe" feasts add up to over 20,000 calories per day for one increasingly large Sumo wrestler!

PACIFIC ISLANDS

1. **Sea Grapes** - throughout the World there are many varieties of grape but "sea grapes" sound a bit strange and definitely out of the ordinary. In the USA particularly Florida there is a small tree, with grape-like fruits called a "sea grape" but this is not our "sea grape". Our ones are found along the coastal waters of the Philippines, Malaysia and Samoa for example, where they are enjoyed as an ingredient in numerous dishes. "Sea grapes" in Japan are seen as a specialist item that comes mostly from Okinawa. However the best "sea grapes" of all are considered by some connoisseurs to be collected by the people of Fiji. If you go east from Brisbane, Australia for 1,700 miles or north from Auckland, New Zealand for 1,300 miles then you are in the right part of the South Pacific to find Fiji. The islands of Fiji add up to over three hundred thereafter someone has to decide when a coral rock is simply a rock or yet another islet. Only two islands are of any size and they are called Viti Levu and Vanua Levu. These islands contain the vast bulk of the population and the capital, Suva, is on Viti Levu (great Fiji). Our "sea grapes" come from a seaweed that thrives in the crystal clear shallow waters around the islands.

The locals forage the grape-like bunches of crunchy spherical bladders they call "nama" to be eaten at home or sold at markets particularly on the large islands. The "sea grapes" are usually eaten raw as part of a fish or vegetable salad or just as a simple side dish with coconut milk. "Nama" pop in your mouth and are very healthy being replete with minerals also rich in vitamins C, E, K, B2 and beta carotene. So why is this seaweed super food not marketed worldwide? Well the seaweed grows in very special niche environment, it is subsistence crop not factory farmed and it is quite perishable with only a 3 day shelf life sad to say.

2. **Break Crust** - my poor French translates the local Tahitian standby known as "casse-croute" to be "brake or bash up crust". Doesn't sound all that appetizing does it? Tahiti is in French Polynesia and is spectacularly beautiful from the inland mountains to the aquamarine lagoons. It is a tourist delight, a paradise with one exception in the form of the strange black beaches here there and everywhere. Reminders that volcanic eruptions way back in time raised the island from the depths or should I say raised two islands that form a rather badly constructed figure of eight. The island has been French for a couple of hundred years so French is the second language after local Tahitian. On the food front their dishes tend to be Polynesian with lots of French influences but also Chinese - the result of a large Chinese population living on Tahiti. Elsewhere in the world, there is a Tunisian 'casse-croute" that is an elongated roll filled with tinned tuna, tomato,

peppers, sliced potato, eggs and North African spices. Our "casse-croute" is a direct result of French food influences on local eating habits. Essentially it is a large baguette packed with almost anything you like but lots of it! They are a common lunch sold at most snack bars and stationary food vans called "roulottes" and the like. There are anorexic ham and cheese versions mostly for the tourists but don't settle for second best go for the proper ones, the locals choose to buy. They are often packed with raw citrus soaked fish and/or coconut milk soaked chicken plus plenty salad. However a monster version might contain strips of fried steak, bacon, cheese, sliced tomato, lettuce and other salad vegetables, a good portion of chips and plenty mayo oozing all over the place. If you go to a "roulotte" and order a monster "casse-croute" take a friend and you might be able to finish it between you.

3. **Stab** - in tagalog, a language spoken by many Filipinos, the word "saksak" has numerous meanings as far as I can tell. It means primarily to stab or pierce but also "saksak" is used in the sense of stuffing clothes into a bag when packing or at least something quite similar to that. It doesn't sound much like anything you would eat though. However if you travel along the coastal regions of Papua New Guinea (PNG to many) you would find the locals consider it as a kind of pudding. No tagalog is not the main, or even a major, language in Papua New Guinea. It turns out that there is a population of Filipino immigrants that live in PNG and between 13 and 15,000 speak tagalog. What do the rest of the

PNG population speak? Well nothing that anyone else understands as far as I can tell any way. We are talking about a country with around 800 spoken languages! I've never been there but can't help thinking how long is their "no entry" sign for instance or "beware of the dog"? Now "saksak" is a traditional dessert in PNG made from pearls of sago mashed up with banana then rapped in banana leaves. Thereafter your pudding is boiled in their ubiquitous coconut milk. Everything about this dish from the sago to the banana and the coconut is reminiscent of the Pacific Islands but why stab? I nave no idea but perhaps "stuffing" banana leaves with things that are tasty is the clue?

4. **Jawbreakers** - no they are from Britain surely? As a child I was brought up partly in England but mostly in Southern Scotland. I was born with a small mouth according to my dentist and a tendency to talk too much according to everyone else. My schoolboy sweetie nemesis was the "gobstopper" or "jawbreaker"; a round rather large and extremely hard confection. The young Grierson was a greedy boy so a large sweet costing little money was irresistible for the journey to school. I could barely get the monster into my small mouth - definitely couldn't talk other than to make slurping or gurgling noises. It was a long walk to school but not long enough to finish off the "jawbreaker" - can't abandon it so late yet again! Sore backside from school even sorer jaw from the "jawbreaker". Now if we travel many thousand miles to the Mariana Islands and their biggest island called Guam then we have another type of 'jawbreaker" but

this is a biscuit not a sweet. These rock-hard biscuits, called "guyuria", are enjoyed by the Chamorro people of the islands and even further afield. The dough is dampened and enriched with coconut milk, blobs of dough are then flattened, ridged and rolled with a fork into a kind of cylindrical shape. The biscuits are deep-fried then wet syrup or dry sugar coated. Once cool and hard, the "jawbreakers" are ready for the family or any visitors. Many Chamorro families feel comfortable only if they have a decent home supply of "guyuria" around in a tin. Now Guam and the USA are closely related to the extent that the islanders have American citizenship. The "jawbreaker" nickname may not be Chamorro but American. After all the US also has "jawbreaker candy" although they tend, unlike the UK equivalent, to have "bubblegum" in the centre. The UK and US sweets are far less common than they once were but Guam "jawbreakers" are just as popular there as ever they were!

AUSTRALIA AND NEW ZEALAND

1. **Snags** - a snag is a short word but over time and in different circumstances it has gained a long list of different meanings. A careless builder leaves behind a new house full of snags but to a fisherman there is the inconvenience of snagging up the fishing line. As a lad I worked for the forestry commission and our snags were tree stumps but to a game keeper a snag is something on a deer's antlers. I remember my mum fretting about snags in her stocking leading to holes but to my daughter, snags are posh tights from Italy! Now if we go all the way to Australia we come across rather tasty snags and this is a local name for sausages. It has been a popular Aussie slang term that has been prevalent since WWII, certainly not before that terrible time. A sausage roll, then and now, is sausage meat in puff pastry whereas a "snag" is an intact cooked sausage that at a barbeque might be rolled up in a single slice of white bread with cooked onions and tomato sauce. I read somewhere that Aussies like their barbeque snags to be cheap and made from fatty beef rather than pork

(the English preference) and that using white bread is essential. Putting their grilled snags, God forbid, into brown bread is simply not the Australian way. Snags in hot dog rolls is also a no-no except in Western Australia but those Aussies are a bit unusual anyway!

2. **Mud Bugs** - they are a delicacy in Australia and are eaten and enjoyed by locals and tourists alike. Though us tourists approach them with a fair amount of concern in the beginning, I know I did. My first plate of "bugs" was up in the "Blue Mountains" outside Sydney. I had a head cold and a long flight from Britain hadn't helped. Friends told me the "Blue Mountain" area was the place to take your cold so as soon as I finished work in Sydney we were off. My nose and head cleared right away, no miracle - simply the blue air of the eucalyptus forests provided masses of tree oil that cleared my head almost immediately. Suddenly I was hungry; when had I last eaten? My Aussie friends were fixated about having "bugs and beer" sounded nasty but you can only die once and I believed I already had! There are two types of "bugs" in Australia, the "Moreton Bay bugs" and the "Balmain" ones we had for the boozy supper. Our "Balmain bugs" inhabit costal waters from Queensland all the way down to Tasmania whereas "Moreton Bay bugs" range over the Northern coastline. They are cooked in many different ways from steaming to barbeque but ours were grilled in garlic butter. You eat the tail meat, which has a rich fishy, lobster-like taste. Indeed restaurants like to refer to them as "slipper lobsters" or even "bay lobsters" in the same way in old school British fish and

chip shops "dogfish" was listed by the fancier name of "rock salmon". Basically when you see "slipper or bay lobster" on an Aussie menu everyone else knows them to be "bugs" or even "mud bugs" although that is also an American name for crawfish! What do you have with bugs? Well a scoop of fries is optional while a mixed salad helps balance the rich bug meat. Neither is essential but lots of beer is the only other requirement!

3. **Hangi** - I was fortunate to once have a temporary job in Auckland, New Zealand for a few months and took my family with me. We stayed in Auckland during the week for work reasons but toured about at weekends in a clapped out but much loved Toyota Corolla. One weekend we set off to a Maori Centre on the "East Cape" of North Island where they were to have a "hangi" and "pakeha" (outsiders) were more than welcome to take part along with the locals. This is a meal cooked in an underground oven consisting of a vast pit that is opened up and rocks placed at the bottom. A huge fire on top heats the rocks to oven temperature, then the meats (pork, beef, chicken, shellfish etc) and vegetables (sweet potato, regular potato, carrots, gourds etc) are placed in the pit. The whole thing is topped with a damp cover including leaves, earthed over and the oven left for several hours to do its work. The food, partly steamed, is not dried out but has a barbeque smokiness - quite unusual, totally delicious. The brilliance of the "hangi" is you all get to help preparing the food, getting the pit ready and so on. You may well have only contributed brute strength and ignorance (under careful but polite

direction) rather than culinary skills but you certainly work up an appetite and make a few new friends in the process. The pit form of cooking is popular on many of the Pacific Islands, although the names differ the fun part is just the same.

4. **Hokey Pokey** - such a very long time ago my mum used to say to me when I had a date "don't get up to any hokey poky with that young lady!" Centuries later I said much of the same thing when my children were teenagers much to their great amusement. "What's Dad on about?" one might say and get the reply from another, "sex I think don't really know it's just Dad?" Back to my mum again and she and dad would do the "hokey cokey" dance with all sorts of strangers in public (under the influence of a sherry and a couple of whiskies but no class A drugs) - "you put your left arm in, your left arm out, in out in out, shake it all about!" - and so it would go on with no limb safe. The same daft song and dance had crossed the Atlantic to the US in the 1940s but there it is the "hokey pokey"! Now in New Zealand it is neither sex nor a silly song, instead it is honeycomb. Not the stuff created by bees but the confection that is surrounded by a thin layer of chocolate in a "crunchy bar". Fry and Sons created crunchy in 1929 and the honeycomb toffee became popular around the World. Personally I loathe "honeycomb", often called "cinder toffee". As a boy tried to eat a crunchy bar an hour or two after having my tonsils removed - the pain went eventually but mentally I'm scarred for life. New Zealand has a long-time enthusiasm for "cinder toffee"

way beyond any other place I know, but they like to call it "hokey pokey". The toffee is made simply by adding baking soda to sugar syrup and indeed my younger kids and their teacher made some at school in a chemistry class. Horrible! They came home with tons of it - I needed counseling. The toffee is eaten naked, coated with chocolate but most popular of all "hokey pokey" is often an addition to vanilla ice cream. "Hokey pokey ice cream" has to be a New Zealand classic and for me just something else crunchy-like to avoid. "Hokey pokey" when applied to "honeycomb" according to Nigella Lawson seems to have originated in Cornwall way back in the distant past. Although I can't imagine any Kiwi believing that.

SOUTH AMERICA

1. **Romeo and Juliet** - over 500 years ago William Shakespeare was writing plays. Many of these gems are all too familiar today to the horror of most schoolchildren and the delight of Shakespeare enthusiasts. For everyone in between, we use bits of Shakespeare in everyday speech - he created over 1,000 new words such as "aerial, assassination, accommodation, bloody, dwindle, frugal, hurry, lapse, lonely, majestic" and many more. The number of Shakespeare created words is "obscene" (and that's his too!). Most of us know a few of the titles of the playwrite's best known plays "Macbeth," "Hamlet" and of course "Romeo and Juliet." We even use Shakespeare phrases, mostly without knowing where they are from. How about "to be or not to be" from "Hamlet" or "fair is foul and foul is fair" from "Macbeth". While from "Romeo and Juliet" comes "parting is such sweet sorrow" and of course "star crossed lovers". Leonard Bernstein by means of his "West Side Story updated "Romeo and Juliet" into 1950s America. At the very least it shows the play's enduring relevance spanning the ages. In Brazil there is a simple but tasty snack or starter they call "Romeu et Julieta". Basically the dish

consists of squares of "guava paste" or in Portuguese "goiabada" and separated by comparably sized squares of locally produced soft, white and salty cheese all held together with a wooden cocktail stick. They are a perfect combination like "Romeo and Juliet" and I guess hence the name. "Guava paste" is a combination of guava and lots of sugar heated up that cools down to form a solid block. It is available in delis, supermarkets and on line and a very decent and practical alternative is quince paste. Getting an appropriate cheese is more difficult but I use "Port Salut" or unripe "brie" that both have the correct texture. There again "halloumi" has its characteristic saltiness that totally offsets the intense sweetness of the sugary "guava paste". Its up to you which cheese you choose but "Romeo and Juliet" is worth a try if you want a different type of nibble.

2. **Tiger's Milk** - I know, you don't get too many tigers in South America outside of a zoo. The apex predatory cats of the South America are the cougar and the puma. Pretty tough characters but not in the same league as the Asian tiger which fortunately for the local wildlife is many thousands of miles away. Even if there were some around (and there are not), other than a most loved baby tiger, no one would be stupid enough to even think about milking a mother tiger. As a result "leche de tigre" has nothing at all to do with any type of tiger known to man. On the other hand surprisingly it has a lot to do with a raw fish dish that is a Peruvian and in general a South American special! That special is called "ceviche" and is the national dish of Peru and also neighbouring

Ecuador. Both these countries are on the Pacific coast of South America above Chile where abundant good quality fish abound. Raw strips of extremely fresh fish and seafood are soused in a sharp acidic fruit juice. Delicate fish get mushy on exposure to sharp fruit juices but firm fish such as "bass", "snapper", "sole", "halibut" and "rock fish" are ideal along with seafood such as "squid", "octopus" and "prawns". Of the fruit juices, it is the sharp ones that are prime additions to your raw fish particularly limes but lemons, sour oranges and pineapples all make the grade. Sliced onions, chopped red chilli and heavy seasoning are essential for any "ceviche". While a range of other vegetables, fruit and herbs can be added to the dish depending on what South American country or region you are in. When the fish and vegetables are eaten, there is the powerful juice left over. It is our "tiger's milk", traditionally served later in a small glass, and is considered by some gourmets as a delicacy even superior to "ceviche" dinner itself.

3. **Little Goat** - our goat comes from Uruguay, in South American terms, a very small country with a population of barely 3 million. It is situated on the Atlantic coast pressed in between its two huge neighbours of Brazil above and Argentina below. In Uruguay "chivito" is a national treasure however the "little goat" turns out to be a humungous sandwich without a trace of goat in any shape or form whatsoever. One story goes that a chef back in the 1940s was asked by customers to roast a goat. It turned out that there were no goats to be had anywhere near at hand. In desperation the chef

made a gigantic sandwich out of everything he had in the kitchen and so the "little goat" was born. Of course we all like to have these kinds of explanatory stories to back up the strange names of some dishes but whether you believe them or not is up to you in the end. Anyway if I was presented with a "chivito" I would expect two doorstep slices of bread or the halves of a really substantial bun. Inside I would look for a mass of ingredients sufficient to feed an army. On the meat side there has to be slices of roast beef although ham and bacon are potential additional extras. Sliced tomato, lots of lettuce leaves, hot stringy mozzarella and a fried egg helps to round off the whole structure. Olives and pickled onions are near at hand while a dip consisting of equal parts of mayo and tomato ketchup is usual (much like "marie rose sauce" that well known dressing from 1960s UK). As you will gather a "chivito" is not designed as a quick nibble just to keep hunger pangs at bay. No it is a calorific monster intended for the starving or the totally indulgent. Pass me another pickle will you?

4. **Hunger Killer** - it is a meaty Argentinian delight. From the gaucho cowboys herding cattle on the plains to the city folks of that country, their meals are dominated by loads of meat. One of my one-time vegetarian sons backpacked around the World and found the most difficult place to eat was Argentina. Certainly Argentinians are acknowledged as the people who eat more meat than anyone else in the South Americas but they are behind Australia and the USA on the World carnivore league table. Non-the-less if you are known

as the "hunger killer" in in Argentina and also it is a national treasure then it has to be a dish on the generous side with a copious amount of meat. The meat in this case is beef; masses of cows are reared in this country although "hunger killer" uses a rather unusual cut called "flank". Not by any means top of every ones shopping list in Britain where it would be called "skirt steak". It is a big, thin section of beef also called "bavette" in French speaking countries. What ever name you use, it is cheap and being quite tender good for "Chinese stir fries", "Mexican fajitas" and the like. Our dish is known locally as "matambre" a combination of the two Spanish words "matar" for kill and "hambre" meaning hunger. The "flank beef" is beaten flat and marinated overnight in vinegar and abundant spice then loaded with peppers, thin sliced carrot, hard-boiled eggs, olives, herbs and other goodies. The meat with its vegetable filling is rolled up, stringed tight and oven baked in a beefy stock rich in onion or just grilled or simply cooked on top of the barbeque (at the Argentinian "asado"). The meat is sliced into rounds with its egg and vegetable stuffing in the middle and eaten warm or cold with potatoes and the classic Argentinian green salsa known as "chimichurra". Actually the filling of a Cornish pasty is a mixture of strips of skirt beef and chopped vegetables so close to also being a "hunger killer".

MEXICO

1. **Drowned Sandwich** - no this isn't a "cheese and pickle special" washed down by a ludicrous number of pints of local beer in an English pub. In Mexico they do their drowning in an entirely different manner. The "drowned sandwich" or more correctly in Spanish the "torta ahogada" is a creation associated with the city of Guadalajara. Underrated as a tourist attraction, few outsiders appreciate that Guadalajara is the country's second city. It is located over 300 miles to the north west of Mexico City and among the facts I did not know about the place is that the town of Tequila is close by so party time! If you want a little music while you drink then Guadalajara is the home of extremely big hats and mariachi bands. All you need now is something to eat surely? I know, how about a very tasty snack to slurp on and I do mean slurp. If you are game then that has to be a decent sized "torta ahogada" perfect to drip on your clothes. It came into existence in the early years of the 20th Century when a "sandwich" salesman dropped a "filled roll" into a vat of "salsa". Rather than waste it the customer ate it and enjoyed it so much he and his friends came back for more. Who can say the story is right or

wrong but the "drowned sandwich" has been around these parts for over 100 years. It consists of a hollowed out crusty "baguette-type of bread" and filled with very tasty "citrus marinated fried pork". The sandwich is partly or completely dunked into a rich "tomato" or a "hot chilli" "salsa" depending on your taste. Dip your sandwich into both if you wish, I would definitely make that choice. The "drowned sandwich" is very much associated with its home city rather like in England a bowl of "scouse" stew is a Liverpool delicacy and on the whole not widely enjoyed around the rest of the country.

2. **Little Donkey** - the "burrito" is possibly one of Mexico's most World famous foods and translates from Spanish as "little donkey". I have a teenage daughter who can't get enough of them so we often go hunting the best burrito when she stays over. Personally I find the "mission burritos" she craves, far too big and messy for me to cope with these days. Burritos are rolled up "tortillas" filled with meat, beans, rice, salad, "guacamole", sour cream, cheese and a host of other things. Vegetarian options are popular (especially with Megan) as is the "breakfast burrito" essentially a cooked breakfast in a wrap. Although you find them in restaurants and franchises, essentially a "burrito" is perfect fast food takeaway fare. Ranging from a sensible cylindrical construction to a humongous sandwich encased in parchment, paper or silver foil (the "mission" variety for example) and sliced in half on the diagonal. Like those mega burgers with all the extras, you have to dislocate your jaw to get any of it into your mouth. Always, at least with

me, there is the lurking possibility that much of the "burrito" will end up in my lap. Although "burrito" I know in Spanish means "little donkey" I think it would be better named "beached whale". Why would Mexicans create such a thing? In truth they didn't. Yes "burritos" came into being in northern Mexico but they were (and still are) modest cigar-like wraps containing a little meat or perhaps cheese and beans. Even today "burritos" are not widespread in their homeland (except for holiday hotspots). It was when they reached the USA in the early part of the 20th Century (and specifically California and Texas) that the "burrito" took on lots of weight, became clothed in tinfoil and morphed into the "mission burrito" we see everywhere in the USA and where ever USA/Mexican cuisine has taken root around the World.

3. **Poisoned Tacos** - you get "tacos" all over the World these days but they are mostly the North American version. The American commercial creations are the soft or crispy "tacos" that inhabit supermarket shelves and last forever. Reputedly they will survive a nuclear holocaust although that seems rather extreme. The crispy tacos were the invention of a US food franchise called Taco Bell who was then able to produce them on an industrial scale. The one place in the World where crispy tacos are not to be found these days is Mexico itself! Mexican tacos are based entirely on freshly made soft "tortillas" that are then rapped around fillings including meats, spices, salad vegetables, sliced peppers, guacamole, sour cream and salsa. Two of the

more famous and unusual Mexican tacos are "tacos Al Pastor" containing marinated pork and pineapple among others and, from Baha, "tacos de pescado" consisting of a flat "tortilla" topped with sour cream, salsa, lettuce and fried fish. The real tacos from Mexico are rather appealing to the taste buds except perhaps "poisoned tacos" (tacos envenenados). "Envenenados" in Spanish means poisoned or contaminated so why would Mexicans, or anyone for that matter, want to eat something with a name like that? Well you wouldn't if it were true however the taco is not poisonous in the least only rather greasy, calorific but very tasty. The recipe for the filling is not all that precise but contains potatoes, beans, sliced onion, chorizo sausage, lots of cheese and a rather fiery red chilli paste. Eat too many and you will feel your arteries start to clog. It seems the name is a bit of a long-term rather than short-term warning about what tastes good doesn't always do you good.

4. **Corn fungus** - actually corn has been cultivated and cropped in Mexico for thousands upon thousands of years. As a result it is more than likely that properly domesticated corn, appropriate for farming rather than just foraging, originated here. A field of corn is really quite attractive especially when the yellow kernels ripen on their cobs. Like any plant, corn is subject to all sorts of disease such as leaf blight, stalk rot, grain mold and many more that confound the best care of the farmer. One of the nasty brigades is a fungus that attacks the young plant and as it grows the fungus develops distinctive and quite unattractive galls. In the US the

"corn fungus" is better known as "corn smut" and something definitely to be avoided or eradicated. On the other hand Mexican farmers are not particularly upset if there is a limited amount of this "corn fungus" and collect the dark galls for home use or selling on. Sounds ridiculous but the ground up fungus galls give an earthy mushroom taste to a number of soups, adds a new dimension to taco fillings and gives quesadillas a lift. This savoury seasoning was not new to Mexico much in the same way that sliced and grated truffles have been a European delicacy for centuries. Since the time of the Aztecs, who called the "corn fungus" by their name of "huitlacoche", the "corn fungus" has enriched the cuisine of Mexican societies then and throughout the ages. The question has arisen, particularly in America, whether "corn smut" might be dangerous if eaten too frequently but the jury is still out on that one. I just have to get my head around this one, I'm used to "smut" on the TV and "smut" from the fire but "smut" on my "taco" seems a bit much!

ELSEWHERE IN CENTRAL AMERICA

1. **Speckled Cock Hen** - it is known in other English speaking countries, notably the USA, as "speckled rooster". A "rooster" has a very obvious and crucial job in the hen house but what to do when the old "cock hen's" best days are over? In rural communities around the World, where meat could not be wasted, the "old cock" or the "eggless hen" might be tough but still was there to be eaten. Slow cook dishes like Scotland's "cock-a-leekie," soup and the rustic "coq au vin" stew from France are key examples of the old bird is note to be wasted. Further slow cook Latin American stews involving "fowl" are tastier made with "rooster" or "old hen" rather than "chicken" which breaks down too much and the same can be said for authentic "Indian curries". Costa Rica lies between Panama to the south and Nicaragua to the north and there they celebrate a dish called "gallo pinto" that is made in almost every home and certainly it is sold in every "cantina" and "sodas" in the country. It is reasonable to consider that this dish consists, at least in part, of an "old bird" past its

best; after all "gallo" is Spanish for "rooster". However it turns out that this is a vegetarian dish. Essentially it consists of "black beans", "cooked white rice", "chopped up onion" and "red peppers" cooked all together with "chopped coriander", some "cumin" and a pinch of "cayenne pepper". The main sauce kick comes from a glug or two from a bottle of "Lizano sauce" ("salsa"). "Lizano" is a factory made bottled sauce used in Costa Rica to bring a bit of zing to dishes while they are being cooked; as such it has similarities to "Worcestershire sauce". Our "meatless speckled cock hen" is flavoursome though not very spicy - indeed Costa Ricans are not into fiery food. Traditionally many locals have their portion of "gallo pinto" as a breakfast special perhaps along with a couple of "fried eggs". Why the name? Well it is down to the colour contrast between the" black beans" and the "white rice" reminding you of Spanish black on white pinto horses and of course those real farmyard "speckled cock hens". Might you be forgiven for saying "when is a "rooster" not a "rooster", when it is "gallo pinto"?"

2. **Red and Spicy** - sounds rather racy but is that just me? In Guatemala however "kak-ik" or "red-spicy" in Mayan is one of their treasured National dishes even to the extent of being named by the Ministry of Culture and Sports as one of Guatemala's heritages. Clearly as it extends back into Guatemala's Mayan past, way before the arrival of the Spanish conquistadors, the claim is entirely justified. The country lies south of Mexico and is still a bit of a wild and rugged place. This land is the home of many volcanoes of which plenty are still active

on a far too regular basis. It is a land of dense jungle, for that matter the name Guatemala may come from an old Mayan word meaning Land of Trees. It is also (all too rightly) proud of its traditions and cultural heritage, as should be the case particularly those that existed before Spanish colonialism. Guatemala gained independence from Spain in the 1820s and had its fair share of political nightmares over the years. However "kak-ik" is more than a tasty dish, it is part of a Nation's food heritage and so carries with it a reverence outsiders don't always appreciate. It is a red soup with "turkey" usually the dark meat of the leg. "Wild turkey" is considered better than domesticated, while the key constituents of the spicy soup are "tomatoes", "peppers", loads of "chilli", plenty "coriander" and local "achiote". The "achiote" is an orange coloured ground spice or paste made from local berries and contributes to the soup's distinctive flavour.

3. **Black Dinner** - this is a dish from the small country of Belize located south of Mexico and to the west is Guatemala. Its coastline is to the east and on the Caribbean sea, festooned with masses of small islands and mangrove swamps. It has British rather than Spanish colonial connections in the past so English is the official language though other languages are common from Mayan to Spanish. Indeed the Mayan connection is strong right through to the local cuisine including the "black dinna" as described locally. Yes I've had all too many black and smoking dinners in my time in hotels, guesthouses and homes where over cooking

is seen as a necessity if not a virtue. There are those that only eat meat rare (the French for instance) and those who revel in everything cremated (too many Scots and Irish I know unfortunately). However Belizean "chimole" is not overcooked only amazingly black. The constituents include a chopped up "chicken", and "pork mince meatballs" with lots of "vegetables" that form a soup that can be thickened with "cornflour". The dish has a characteristic black colour because of a Mayan spice blend rich in "smoked chillies" known as "black Ricardo" mix. The black of the meaty soup contrasts with plentiful supply of "tortillas", a substantial bowl of "boiled rice" and sliced quarters of "hard boiled egg" scattered around. All are obligatory extras for this dish that often makes a special appearance in Belize around Christmas time.

4. **Three Milks** - you may think the dish reads like it should be a special industrial dairy product. On the other hand, how about it being a complicated concoction to be sipped carefully at a probiotic health farm as an alternative to steak and chips? Fortunately it is neither of those horrors but instead it is a really calorific and gooey cake to be eaten sparingly but to be enjoyed thoroughly. Definitely not to be missed if an opportunity beckons. Our cake is no obscure regional fancy but it is eaten all over South America, Central America and the Southern half of the USA. As is the case for many popular dishes, the origins of "three milks cake" is subject to many claims and counter claims but most likely it first came into existence in Nicaragua though Mexico would put up a

strong counter argument to that assertion. Certainly it is more popular in those two countries than anywhere else in the region. Every café and cake shop in Mexico and Nicaragua would produce their own versions as being the best to be found. If Nicaragua is the place to go to taste "pastel de tres leches" what is like? Even in its place of birth, the cake tends to vary quite considerably from place to place. Certainly around the Latin American World it tends to look quite different depending where you are. Essentially however it is a sponge cake with a heavily whipped cream topping. To the sponge dough is added a mixture of cream, evaporated milk and condensed milk ("three milks"). As a result when cooked the sponge is moist (if no butter is included) and never crumbly. Condensed and evaporated milk are available Worldwide as canned products but they are particularly popular in warm countries because of their long shelf lives. Evaporated milk is a milk concentrate while condensed milk is a sweetened concentrate. They combine with cream to create the tastiest sponge cake that you could possibly imagine. Take a cup of strong coffee and a slice of "pastel de tres leches"- sponge, thick layer of heavily whipped cream and some sliced strawberry. Enjoy them both in Central America or at home, tastes great either place.

CUBA

1. **Fried** - is a uniquely Cuban burger known locally as the "frita Cubana" or just simply "frita" meaning "fried". We all know that the burger is America's top food item. German immigrants in New York and Chicago introduced the locals to what they called the "hamburger steak". It being a patty of "beef mince", "breadcrumbs" and "chopped onion" served on a plate with "potatoes", "vegetables" and "thick gravy". The "burger" only became street food that could be eaten on the move when the "beef patty" was first placed between "slices of bread" (the "bun" was a later modification). All of this was happening at the beginning of the 20th Century. Quite early on in the evolution of the burger, in fact in the 1920s, Americans introduced the "beef patty sandwich" to Cuba. Having a vibrant food culture they soon came up with a version of their own that they called the "frita". As we all know, the classic American version is a "grilled beef patty" in a "bun" topped with "sliced tomato", "chopped lettuce", a raw "onion ring", "pickle" and "relish". The "frita" is a "patty of beef" but also with "pork mince" or "chorizo sausage" and "garlic", "cumin" and "smoky paprika". The meat is

pan cooked rather than flame grilled then stuffed in a "toasted bun" packed with "thin fries" and "onion". The "tomato sauce" has "Cuban spices" plus "chilli" to give a kick. The "frita" was sold in stalls all over Cuba but was effectively lost to that Island when Castro came to power and subsistence living was the norm. However the "frita" survived from the 1960s onwards in Miami and Florida with those masses of Cuban exiles. Today with tourism returning you can get a "frita" in its country of origin but the biggest and best "Cuban burgers" are still to be had in Little Havana, Miami and they are really special I think.

2. **Midnight** - this is a tale of two mega sandwiches both with a Cuban connection. The first is the "Cuban sandwich" while the second is "midnight" or in Spanish it is the "medianoche". I used to go to the Tampa Bay area of Florida most years for a week or so. The first thing I wanted after a long flight was a "Cuban sandwich;" surely I've got my geography wrong? Not a bit of it, the home of the "Cuban sandwich" is Tampa! Sure it was created to feed Cuban workers in Tampa towards the beginning of the 20th Century but it is American through and through. It consists of a rather crusty baguette filled with sliced marinade pork, ham, salami (Italian connection strong in the Bay area), Swiss cheese, pickles, mustard and mayonnaise. All tasty components with nothing delicate - designed to fill working people and one greedy Scots tourist! It has now gone over to Cuba but it did not start life there. Now that is not the case for "midnight" that sandwich

did originate in Cuba mostly to give, in pre communist times, revelers something to snack on when they leave the wild clubs and bars of Cuba's cities. The customers would arrive late at night - hence the name "midnight". The bread roll is also elongated but soft, while the filling consists of sliced citrus-infused pork and ham (both are Cuban favourites), local cheese, pickles and sauces. When "medianoche" travelled to Miami with Cuban exiles, it became larger and almost indistinguishable from the Miami version of the "Cubano sandwich" (that has no salami in that City) except the former is based on soft and the latter on crusty bread. It may be the two delicious sandwiches will become indistinguishable from each other but they originated 500 miles apart in two different Worlds.

3. **Old Clothes** - Personally I love my old clothes so I am not so keen on new ones. Don't get me wrong I do buy new stuff but when it comes to coats, jackets, trousers and shoes I have issues. They are all kind of stiff, unyielding and not at all homely if you get what I mean? I've been known to leave a new top or jacket for a couple of years before I get round to wearing it. My old treasured friends were in fashion when the dinosaurs roamed the planet and mysteriously the more unsightly end up in the bin - now how does that happen? My family says my really ancient clothes just lose the will to live and commit suicide - not too sure I believe them. It's a no brainer that once a foodie guy like myself heard of a dish called "ropa vieja" then it has to be intriguing to say the least. It is an absolute special

in Cuba where "skirt (flank) beef" is the key feature of the dish ("skirt" is popular in Latin America - see South America and "hunger killer" earlier). The "beef" is cooked up quickly and shredded then mixed with "tomatoes", "red peppers", "onions", "stoned olives" and "capers" including loads of "paprika". Its usual partners on a plate are a mound of white rice and a portion of beans. It is Cuban to the core but actually originated far away in the Canary Islands where it was (and still is) a popular home and cafe dish enjoyed by many including myself. In the Canaries and Southern Spain however the dish differs by having "chickpeas" and "cooked potatoes" added in with the "shredded beef". The rest of the dish requires "peppers", "onions", "olives" and "paprika" as is the case in Cuba. "Ropa vieja" is wide ranging throughout Spanish-speaking countries not always called by that name. In Guatemala for instance the dish is known as "hilachas" or "threads" and it is a meal that is enjoyed everywhere in that country. Our "old clothes" might have originated among the Sephardi communities of Spain but I prefer the Cuban version. My belief is that tasty strips of "quick grilled beef" go perfectly with a mound of "boiled rice" and "cooked beans". They are far better partners for "old clothes" than "chickpeas" and "potatoes"!

4. **Cornet** - I come from a long line of ice cream fanciers, that continues to this day and includes my children mostly grown up now. It must be a genetic thing not helped in my case by living at times in the Wirral (New Brighton) and at other times in Southport. Ice cream

parlours abound in both places. You can eat your selected ice in a bowl, a cup, a tub or even as a wafer I suppose but this ultimate dissert really comes into its own in a cone or cornet. Edible cornets for ice cream and soft disserts have been around in Europe since Victorian times but they were manufactured in bulk in the USA from 1912 onwards. Further back in time, inedible cornets were created to hold all manner of goodies and sweetmeats. The tradition still continues in many parts of the World including Cuba. Here they have a cornet constructed from a palm leaf that has contents that are a delicious mixture of for example pineapple, coconut, cane sugar and honey. Alternatively it might consist of a paste made from coconut and coconut water mixed with almonds and honey. When Christopher Columbus first arrived in Cuba he landed in what was to become Baracoa city Nothing to do with Columbus however but our palm leaf confection originates in Baracoa where it is called "cucurucho". It turns out, the city is situated on Honey Bay so its not surprising that the multitude of diverse "cucurucho" fillings all seem to have honey as a common ingredient.

JAMAICA

1. **Festival** - The island of Jamaica is a place of music, religion, food and fun. Despite being a little country of less than 3 million people, it has such a huge influence on the World's popular and cultural music. Way back it was Calypso, followed by Ska, then the massive Reggae movement followed by all sorts of other music developments including Dancehall. Music, some religion and loads of fun are integral to the many events. The island has a full yearly program of celebrations and festivals to enjoy that cover diverse eclectic events from Independence Day or Labour Day to Reggae Sumfests or Jerk Festivals. Lots of formal and informal get togethers - real fun affairs as is the Jamaican way but our "festival" may well be an important attendant at all or many of these but it isn't a festival event but something you eat! Just as "proper" festivals are an intrinsic way of Jamaican life, the "festival" is a cornmeal bread that is an essential component of a huge range of Jamaican meals especially the classic ones. Every Jamaican get together, whether it be in Jamaica, UK, USA, Costa Rica or where ever, "festival" always will be there in considerable abundance. The breads go

well with "jerk chicken", Jamaican "fruit and vegetable salads", "ackee and saltfish" and almost everything else. Basically "festival" is a fried combination of flour, cornmeal and baking powder with a little sugar and spices like cinnamon. To my way of thinking "festival" is a close relative of the South American "Johnny cake" and the North American "hushpuppy". Why call them "festival"? Well when eating them, you bring a festival to your mouth of course!

2. **Vital** - English can be a difficult language because multiple words can mean the same thing more or less and also a single word can have multiple meanings. Such is the case with "vital" that in one context means essential or much needed while alternatively it can mean energetic or lively as would be the case with vitality. If that were not enough then our "vital" is a stew usually referred to with the first letter dropped as "ital." There are numerous Jamaican stews but "ital." is unashamedly vegetarian. When my eldest three, now very grown up adults, were teenagers, two were vegetarian and one a carnivore. An "ital" recipe from a Jamaican friend came in very handy because the basic recipe is so versatile. I could make big bowls of vegetable stew for the vegetarians and give a smaller side dish to the carnivore with meat or fish - job done! As you would expect, an Island recipe is dominated by local vegetables such as "cho cho", "dasheen", "sweet potato", "yam", "ladies fingers (okra)", "plantain", "pumpkin" and the like whereas in England more northern vegetables such as "swede", "leeks", "potato", "cauliflower" and so

forth often substitutes for the more exotic vegetables. Some recipes will have "lentils" or "kidney beans" and even "dumplings" as fillers. A "scotch bonnet chilli", "thyme", "curry powder", "allspice", "turmeric" and "coconut milk" with "onions" and "tomato" complete the stew. It is a Rastafarian creation so light on salt and rich in herbs and spices is the key to a good "ital."

3. **Stamp and Go** - It is a very oddly named fritter sold by Jamaican roadside vendors. When we Brits think of fritters it is usually the apple variety that comes to mind or, if in a Chinese restaurant, a banana fritter with syrup is usually prominent on the dissert menu. However all sorts of foods from vegetables to meats or even seafood can be battered and deep-fried into fritters. In India there are "pakoras", Japan has its "tempora", France has sweet "beignets" and the USA has "spam fritters". Our Jamaican "stamp and go" usually but not exclusively contains salt cod. The sales are at their highest at breakfast time but it is also eaten throughout the rest of the day as a tasty snack. I associate salt cod with European tastes and those of Portugal, Spain, Italy and Scandinavia in particular. Historically the fishermen who fished far away from costal waters needed to preserve their catch also if the fish needed to go inland it needed to remain edible for a long time. The solution was air-drying and/ or salting. This became even more of an issue when a vast stock of fish, mostly cod but also other species, was found off the coast of Newfoundland in the 17th Century. The abundant fishing on the Grand Banks took "salting cod" to an industrial scale. A fast harvest

of cheap protein came to Europe over hundreds of years. The dark side was that masses of "salt cod" also went to the Caribbean and South America to feed the masses of slaves on the plantations and effectively fueled that dreadful human exploitation! The aftermath has been a liking for "salt cod" all over the Americas particularly Jamaica - "ackee and salt cod" is a national dish. "Stamp and go" has been around since the 18th Century when those impatient British sailors off their sailing ships would be impatient waiting for their Jamaican fritters, they would stamp their feet with frustration and off they would go!

4. **Hummingbird Cake** - if you are a cake lover then you cannot fail to like "hummingbird". It is a great cake so much so that other countries, like the USA, like to claim it as theirs but it is originally Jamaican to the last crumb. How did the controversy arise? Well it seems to be down to the Jamaican Tourist Board and a lady from the Deep South. At the start of the 1970s Jamaica wanted to attract more American tourists to their island so as part of the campaign the Tourist Board released a set of Jamaican recipes that included "hummingbird cake" and Americans took a liking to this new cake. A far greater impact came from Mrs L.H. Wiggins who published her recipe for Hummingbird cake in the Southern Living Magazine in 1978. It soon became the magazine's most requested recipe ever! As a result the recipe and variants were being made in homes all over the USA and reproduced in American recipe books thereafter. Mrs Wiggins never explained the name nor

from where the recipe came. For that matter no one has been able to contact or interview her over the years. In America at least the assumption was that our Jamaican traditional cake was native to the southern USA. The Jamaican "hummingbird cake" is named after the swallow tailed humming bird, the National emblem of Jamaica. Locally the bird is known affectionately as the doctor bird, actually as it happens an alternative name for our cake! Jamaican versions combine orange juice, mashed banana and crushed pineapple into the cake mix giving the whole thing a fruity taste and a moist texture when baked. The cake is often topped with nuts and a wash of hot jam or jelly. Cream toppings are adopted sometimes but only sparingly. On the other hand in the USA the cake is often multilayered and smothered with cream cheese frosting, not in the least traditional.

OTHER CRIBBEAN ISLANDS

1. **Doubles** - are associated with the islands of Trinidad and Tobago particularly Trinidad. Together with a few additional small islands they make up the country of Trinidad and Tobago situated towards the end of the Caribbean island chain close to South America. The islands were at one time British owned we wanted them not for their beauty but to establish cotton and sugar plantations. These open-air sweatshops had a hierarchy where African slaves did all the work and plantation managers did all the shouting. When slavery was banned someone came up with the idea of the indentured labourer. People from far and wide, but mostly India and South East Asia, flocked to the islands for the promise of free land following five years plantation work. The work was grim, subsistence living and plantation managers still did all the usual shouting. The exploitation did have interesting consequences on the islands' demographics. The ethnicity of the two predominant Trinidadian groups are more or less equal in numbers - descendants from African slaves and Indo-Trinidadians originating

during indenture times. It is from the latter culture that "doubles" arose. Essentially it is "channa (chickpea) curry" with cucumber chutney, relish, hot sauce and the like sandwiched between two cooked "barra flatbreads." The "barra fried flatbread" and "chickpea curry" was around since the Asian Indians arrived way back in the 19th Century but "doubles" only came into being in the 20th Century in the 1930s. Being a "double" it became a "channa and chutney sandwich" and able to be eaten on the move so now it was street food and a tasty mobile snack. The innovators of Indian extract took time to get their creation established but now it is a must have food if you visit the islands of Trinidad and Tobago for work or pleasure.

2. **Wrapped Children** - a mum says to her children, "wrap up well, it's wet outside!" Well I suppose it depends on what part of the World you are in and in this case our "wrapped children" come from the Dominican Republic. The Republic shares the large island of Hispaniola with its smaller neighbour Haiti to the west. Further west of Haiti is Jamaica and Cuba while to the east of the Dominican Republic is Puerto Rico. The language of the country is Spanish so the "wrapped children" are "ninos envueitos". Of course we are not dealing here with actual children for this dish but a mixture of cooked rice and savoury mince. The mince, usually beef, is made more interesting by mixing in ground garlic, fine chopped onion and red pepper plus added seasoning. The mince needs browning off in a pan then, when cooled, it is folded into the cooked rice.

Portions of the filling, the children are "wrapped" up in par cooked cabbage leaves. The parcels are then placed on a baking dish and stewed in a piquant tomato sauce. "Stuffed cabbage rolls" are common in World cuisine however they are mostly associated with Eastern Europe (Germany, Poland, Hungary, Czech Republic, Ukraine, Russia and the like), Balkans (Romania, Serbia, Bosnia and Montenegro, Greece and others) and the Middle East (Israel, Turkey, Lebanon, Syria, Palestine, Iraq and even more). Clearly there is nothing odd about "stuffed cabbage rolls" except that they are enjoyed so much in a specific Caribbean country. It seems a wave of immigrants arrived in the Dominican Republic from the Middle East in the 19th Century bringing an enthusiasm for "cabbage rolls" with them. There are other "ninos envueitos" in the Spanish-speaking world including a Chilean dish of "steak wrapped around vegetables" while in Mexico and other places it is a tasty "ham and cheese rollup" in white bread or even a "Swiss roll"-like creation. As far as I know, nowhere other than the Dominican Republic however is there a "stuffed cabbage roll" called ominously "wrapped children".

3. **Oil Down** - it is the national dish of Grenada, which is a small island group in the Caribbean. Not to be confused with the large city in Spain, Granada, spelled slightly differently. The British at one time knew Grenada as their island of spice because it has the climate and soil conditions ideal for growing the treasures of the Spice Islands of South East Asia. Even today going around Grenada's main islands there are a plethora of different

spices to be found. Indeed tiny Grenada is one of the main producers of nutmeg in the World. Grenadians, in line with all the Caribbean Islanders, like to party so barbeques and cookouts are everywhere and sometimes on a town or village-wide scale. There will be various delights at such events but the National dish of "oil down" is an essential. You don't make "oil down" for one or two - it is for a crowd of people and often made by several temporary chefs all having a good time together. "Salt fish" is an essential but there are other meats like "salt pork" and "conch" that bulk up the dish. "Salt fish" and "salt pork" need soaking overnight. Along with the salt meat and/or seafood, it is usual to include chopped up "breadfruit", "sliced dasheen root", a few "carrots", "celery", "onions", "peppers" and "dasheen leaves" on top. It all cooks down in its drum or giant pot with herbs like "chives", "parsley" and "thyme" and spices like "chilli", "turmeric", "ginger" and, of course, more than a little "nutmeg". The liquid for the pot is a heady mix of "oil", "coconut milk" and "cream" integrated with the spices. While simmering away, the spicy sauce sticks to the vegetables and some "oil" sinks to the bottom of the stew creating what the locals call an "oil down" effect. Tuck in everyone!

4. **Goat Water** - now we are at the western end of Hispaniola in the country of Haiti. Not a big country but one with a turbulent history and spooky associations. Towards the end of the 18th Century the slaves in the land of Saint Dominique, as Haiti was once called, conducted an effective revolution against their French masters and

took over the country. I guess few today know of this landmark victory for the oppressed but at the time it terrified the slaveholders throughout the World. To deal with the situation Haiti was isolated from the World at large and rumour mongering was encouraged especially if it involved voodoo priests, zombies and ungodly activities. Zombie myths still linger with us stoked up by films, books and even occasional newspaper articles but these days the myth perpetuation is more to do with ignorance and misconception than malice. Although Haiti is no island paradise, quite the opposite. Dictatorship, corruption and gang-related intimidation have seen to that. Malnutrition has been all too common and I understand it is still rife. What then is "goat water" - some pond for domestic animals to drink or a fluid used by a voodoo priestess perhaps? It is neither, instead it turns out to be a rather nutritious soupy stew based on goat meat! It isn't prime, what is cooked are all sorts of chopped up bits of goat with bones and all. An array of herbs and spices plus plenty substantial vegetables like yam and potato complete the dish. I have made it sound like a make-do dish although that is not the case it is a slow cook dinner. Indeed it is revered on many of the Caribbean islands as well as Haiti itself. "Goat water" is highly nutritious and equivalent to for example "bone broth" in terms of its suspected health benefits. Our soup has legendary aphrodisiac qualities according to many in the Caribbean, to the extent it is often on the menu at weddings.

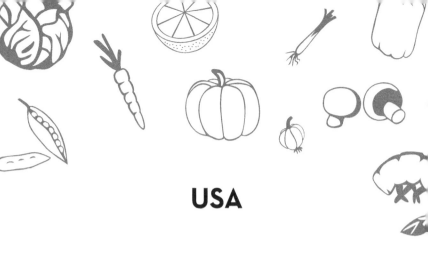

USA

1. **Rocky Mountain Oysters** - they are calf and bull testicles deep-fried so nothing much to do with either mountains or oysters really. I've seen them on menus in North Texas, which is the "heart" of cattle country in the Southern States and North Texas has "Rocky Mountain oyster" festivals now and then. However the cowboy home of the "Rocky Mountain oyster" is further west in Colorado after all as a state it is smack up against the Rockies. No matter where you are in those beef enthusiastic states, "rocky oysters" look a bit like bizarre shaped chicken nuggets because they are egg washed then crumb coated and deep-fried. So do beware if you are one of the unwary at a buffet your "nugget" may be an "oyster". There is another oyster but from the prairies rather than the mountains. A "prairie oyster" is a hang over cure, therefore if you have had too much to drink the night before remember to stay in the prairie and avoid the mountainous heights! Mind you since the prairie oyster consists of raw egg, spices and vinegar - both the prairie and mountain version is best avoided by all but the desperate or the ridiculous. Although I have to

say that in my youth I was an unfortunate competitor in a "prairie oyster" speed drinking competition - very messy! I have managed to avoid the nasty "Rocky Mountain" boys though, left them well alone. Can't be too boastful on that front however but that was on the other side of the Atlantic! I was minding my own business in a bar in Hungary with a strong beer, it was a bit too strong so best I should eat something. I turned down the toasts smothered with dripping also the pig's feet stew and settled for their rather neat little pies. The pastry and rich gravy was nice but the meat was a bit odd. I had spent decades avoiding the "Rocky Mountain" version of testicles but I've always been a sucker for a pie. Oh dear I found that to be a dreadful mistake! When I knew my pie was calf testicle, the beer didn't taste quite so strong as I desperately cleared my throat.

2. **Hot Dogs** - we are so familiar with this form American street food that we no longer think the name is strange. Essentially it is a sausage in an elongated bun with toppings and relishes. The type of sausage used then and now came to America with immigrants from central Europe, the "frankfurter" (Germany) and the "wiener" (Austria). The "frankfurter" was essentially pork in Germany but became predominantly beef in its new homeland of America. These tasty sausages were immensely popular especially in the North although at this time they were without their characteristic elongated bun or any bread at all for that matter. The name "hot dog" is possibly borrowed from Germany

where "frankfurters" and their like had been called dachshund or little-dog sausages for hundreds of years. In the USA, "frankfurters" in bread were on sale in New York towards the end of the 19th Century but the shot in the arm was selling "hot dogs" and other snacks at baseball games. The "long roll" is said to have come into its own at the St Louis World Fair in 1904 although this claim is refuted by food historians who think the "roll's" take over bid was more gradual. It also took time for the full range of toppings to become established. Ah! Those marvelous toppings - "mustard", "tomato ketchup", "mayo", "relish", "chilli beef", "fried onions", "melted cheese" and all the rest. I love all of them except for "chilli beef". My last ever "chilli dog" was in London many years ago, I was admiring my lunch then tripped and the whole thing "bun", "dog", "chilli beef" and "mustard" slipped unerringly into a posh lady's Harrods bag. God what an absolutely gooey mess it made and the more I apologized to the lady the more incensed she became - nasty very nasty! Mind you that could be said of "hot dogs" in general accidents aside - the best quality ones are brilliant but the worst reach a level of artificialness that is quite disgusting. Mind you great, foul or in between the American people get through twenty billion "hotdogs" per year and that is only one country's intake of this World wide junk food phenomenon.

3. **Poor Boy with Debris** - unfortunately there are all too many poor boys and girls in this World while debris is just a rather pretentious word for rubbish or waste

as far as most people are concerned. However in the USA "debris" can be another thing all together and in one sense is far from being rubbish rather it is without doubt a brilliant tasty "gravy" or dipping "jus". To make a decent "gravy" you need all the good bits at the bottom of a roasting pan thickened with flour or some such over heat and then mixed with stock (a close relative of Yorkshire's "mucky dripping" see earlier). On the other hand a "jus" has all sorts of tasty add ins but it is not thickened. In Britain a "jus" would just be called a "thin gravy". In New Orleans they take a "shoulder (chuck) of beef" and just simmer it in rich stock, containing "chopped vegetables", "sliced onion", "Worcestershire sauce", "hot sauce" and "Cajun spices", for many hours until the meat is falling apart. The "chuck" is set aside and sliced - a messy business because the meat tends to shred. That is fine because all the meaty scraps go into the "jus" to make, with extra simmering and thickening, "debris". "Sliced beef" along with "lettuce" and "mayo-mustard sauce" are packed into a crusty "baguette-type" "elongated roll" to become the "poor boy" sandwich - or more accurately "po'boy". The "debris" is an essential extra for dunking the roll and making it more delicious (see earlier the "drowned sandwich of Mexico). This is nothing like your standard "roast beef sandwich", this is economy grub but to many even more delicious. I am told "po'boys" were first created to feed striking streetcar workers in 1920s New Orleans and the sandwiches needed to be filling and economical - they are that and more but also delicious. The "po'boy sandwiches" need not be "beef" (though often are) - "deep fried chicken", "battered prawns" ("shrimp" in the US), "oysters" and "crab" are perfect alternatives. I am particularly partial to a crispy "battered shrimp po'boy" with loads of "lettuce" and "spicy mayo" - heaven in a "bun"!

4. **Grits** - most of what I have written about is to my taste and delicious but there are exceptions. I freely admit, like many folks, to having an aversion to the various dishes of animals' private parts like "Rocky Mountain oysters" (above) or "dragon in the flame of desire" (see China earlier). They do have interesting names but that is as far as it goes. On the slightly less exotic front, Welsh laverbread is enjoyed by many, takes a bit of getting used to for some but for me I never will - it is truly horrible! However you can if you wish drop to another level altogether! I spent much of my working life going several times a year to the Southern States of America. I absolutely love the food in these States from Cajun dishes in Louisiana, to barbeque steaks in Texas and then on to a bowl of chilli in New Mexico - brilliant as long as there is no hotdog (see earlier)! Although there is a real nasty to be had along the way in all these places and it is called "grits"! The name is enough to put you off but no, somewhere in Southern US DNA, there is a compulsion to gulp down "corn goop". The native American Indians have thrived on "grits" for centuries and in a fiendishly cunning move they introduced a bowl of "grits-like mush" to the colonists in Virginia. It shows how desperate those people were that they quite liked the indigenous dish. Basically "grits" are "ground

corn" or "hominy" (alkali processed corn) cooked with plenty "butter" and "cream". Grit in modern English can mean strength of character or an alternative name for gravel whereas in old English it was a term for "coarsely ground cereal". There are similarities in texture between American "grits" and Italian "polenta" but they are far from being identical and to me at least taste completely different. One being atrocious the other sublime!

CANADA

1. **Jiggs' Dinner** - what on earth is a Jiggs when it is at home? Well thankfully you don't have to eat one because it turns out that in the eastern Canadian state of Newfoundland there once was a local comic strip called "Bringing up Father." The main character was an Irish man called Jiggs. You have to go back a bit for this comic strip, Jiggs was at his best in the early decades of the 20th Century but he still lives on in the form of his favourite meal - then and now called the "Jiggs' Dinner". We are not dealing with the exotic, it is simply a good dinner consisting of "cured beef", perhaps a "hen", "potatoes", "cabbage", "turnips" and "carrots". Fine dining it is not but a decent comfort meal consisting of filling hot food for a cold climate to be enjoyed with family and friends it is with out doubt. On Sunday in "St Johns" the capital and other towns in Newfoundland the "Jiggs' dinner" is the main item on the menu of numerous hotels and restaurants. If it is for a big party, then the whole meal is served on a giant plate so every one can help them selves to what they like best. If this feast was not enough, a really substantial old school steamed pudding called a "duff"

rounds off the whole Sunday dinner. To me the whole "Jiggs' dinner" event whether a Sunday lunch or at some other event is definitely old school in the extreme. However old school it may be but there are numerous old school dishes around the World celebrated by many but perhaps not admired by all. I'm thinking of "pot-au-feu" that is a French National treasure though in essence it is a simple "cuts of beef," "onion", "leek", "potato" and "root vegetable" "stew." How about the Scots and their "Burns supper" almost a local legend but just "haggis", "swede" and "mash" plain fare indeed. Further a Danish lunch at home would not be complete were there not a plate of "pickled herring", "onion", "capers" and "raw egg" with "rye bread" on the side. "Jiggs and his supper" can hold his head high among these guys.

2. **Beavers Tails** - beavers are to be found on the waterways of Canada as they are in other countries. However they are a mascot of that Country even although at one time they were almost wiped out. The beaver's skill is to cut down trees and branches to dam streams and make their lodges. Essentially they alter their surrounding environment and engineer it to suit their specific needs. Seems a bit like us doesn't it? They have these amazing sticky out teeth adapted for chewing wood. Their well-used teeth get a battering but continue to grow through out life. The beaver has another great asset and that is an extraordinary tail! The animal itself is all fur except its tail has scales like a snake. It is a ridiculous size compared to the

beaver's body and is a fantastic steering device. The tail is a weird but distinctive paddle-shaped appendage. A shape that in the Canadian capital of Ottawa was copied by Grant and Pam Hooker back in the 1970s to create their distinctive bread pastries kind of like Scottish "bannocks". The Canadian dough creation is deep fried and served hot, wrapped in paper. The couple sold their "beavers tails" freshly made at local markets and fairs. Over the years they took off to the extent that they are now countrywide. The original classic toppings for "beaver tails" are "sugar" and "cinnamon" or "butter and jam" - very tasty, very simple. These days however your Canadian "beavers tail" is topped by almost everything you can imagine and a few things you might not expect. On the sugary side "chocolate spread" is common, "honey" works well, as does "peanut butter" while melted "chocolate bars" with a scattering of "sugary sweets" takes the "tail" to another level. "Beaver tails" also come in the form of a savoury alternative with "melted cheese" or "ham and cheese" at the top of the list however you can smarten your "tail" up with "shrimp (prawns)" perhaps even "lobster" or dumb it down with "fries" and "ketchup". Whatever you favour, "beaver tail" is a must have dish on a visit to Canada these days.

3. **Persians** - no we haven't jumped back to the Middle East for these treats nor are they anything to do with spoilt fluffy round-faced cats. It happens to be the case that our "Persians" are rather special "donut-type" delicacies that originated in Thunder Bay. It is a small

city of not much more than 100,000 people, which is situated on the western shores of Lake Superior. For those visitors who go to Thunder Bay there are many activities to undertake since it is undoubtedly a place of historical interest. In addition the City is surrounded by countryside of quite outstanding natural beauty. On your list of "must do" activities there might be museums, art galleries, markets, boating trips, nature trails and a host of other options when visiting the Thunder Bay area. Although top of many tourists' activity lists would be to go to one or other of the "Persian Man" outlets either the restaurant or the café. Dearie me this essential excursion is nothing to do with "kebabs", "biryani", "pilau rice" or "flatbreads" but everything to do with getting a misshapen "cinnamon donut" smothered with vibrant "pink icing". Our "Persian" came into being back in the middle years of the 20th Century in the hands of a baker called Art Bennett. The Bennett bakery was (and still is) the epicentre for the production of "Persians" in the city. It seems "Persians" have a reputation far beyond Thunder Bay that extends throughout Canada and parts of North America. There are variants you can get in a number of places but the Thunder Bay recipe is a secret having only been passed down to subsequent owners of the Bennett Bakery by Bennett himself. Why call them "Persians"? It's not entirely clear but a well known American general called Pershing from WWI visited Bennett at Thunder Bay so "Persian" might be a corruption of his name "Pershing" but as a reliable explanation it is a bit thin.

4. **Big Turk** - we go from "Persians" to a "Turk" but still we are not really in the Middle East. I clapped eyes on our "big Turk" for the first time, not in Turkey but in a sweet shop located inside an underground mall in Toronto! There it was - a Nestle confectionary product, not sold in the USA, unknown in the UK nor is it found anywhere else I know of. Even in Nestle's home location of Switzerland it is not to be found anywhere. The "big Turk" is a "chocolate-covered" confection bar with a firm, jelly-like filling separated into bite sized segments ambitiously described as "Turkish delight". If you have eaten genuine "Turkish delight" at any time definitely don't go looking for a "big Turk" to give you the same experience. No the "Turk" is quite, quite different - nothing wholesome and plenty artificial about this "delight". The segmented contents that make up the "big Turk" bar lurking beneath the "chocolate coating" is something entirely alien but comfortably familiar at least to me. My mother had two great food pals, "cashew nuts" at Christmas and "Fry's Turkish delight" bar at any time of the year. Now this British "Turkish delight" confection and the "big Turk" are chocolate-coated siblings. Different shapes but each containing the semi-solid lurid red stuff that looks like the aftermath of a failed experiment conducted by a mad chemist. I am of sufficiently mature years to remember "Steve McQueen's" very first film where he had the starring role in "The Blob". Not the best of titles I have to say but descriptively accurate. A vividly "red jelly" monster slithered around eating folks not sure how that happened because panicking people ran very fast while

"The Blob" slithered ever so slowly but that is movie magic isn't it? The "big Turk" is a collection of little "red jelly monsters" trapped in "chocolate". Perhaps the McQueen giant blob roves around looking for revenge because of all those sweet-toothed Canadians eating its "chocolate" covered babies perhaps?